The Substitute
Michael Skelton

THE SUBSTITUTE
Copyright © Serpent Club Press, 2017
All rights reserved

No part of this book may be used or reproduced in any manner whatsoever without written permission except in the case of brief quotations embodied in critical articles and reviews.

For more information please contact
Serpent Club Press at editor@serpentclub.org

Serpent Club Press books may be purchased for educational, business, or sales promotional use. For more information please contact
Serpent Club Press at editor@serpentclub.org

Second Edition
First printed in 2015 by Serpent Club Press.

Printed in the United States of America
Set in Williams Caslon
Designed by Emily Gasda

ISBN
9780990664376

LCCN
2015957263

The Substitute

OTHER BOOKS BY SERPENT CLUB PRESS:

Autumn, Again; Spring, Anew
Michael Skelton & Stephen Morel

A Quarter Century
Eda Gasda

Circumambulate
Daniel Bossert

Moon on Water
Matthew Gasda

New Writing: Volume I

New Writing: Volume II

On Bicycling: An Introduction
Samuel Atticus Steffen

Sonata for Piano and Violin
Matthew Gasda

What Was Left Of The Stars
Claire Åkebrand

CONTENTS

one
DEMOCRACY

two
MYSTICISM

three
UN-EDUCATION

four
FRAGMENTS

texts cited

acknowledgments

For democratic artists

one DEMOCRACY

[T]hese principles—democracy, equality, individual freedom and universal justice—now move us as articles of faith. Holding them sacred, we act (or fail to act) in their names. And in the freewheeling fashion of words that are summoned up to name the ideal, they prod us ceaselessly toward the refinement and perfection of those formulations of policy and configurations of social forms of which they are the signs and symbols... They interrogate us endlessly as to who and what we are; they demand that we keep the democratic faith.

—Ralph Ellison, 'The Little Man at Chehaw Station'

On Walt Whitman

1

In 'Democratic Vistas,' Walt Whitman's essay on the future of aesthetic democracy in America, Whitman subtly transposes lines from poems in *Leaves of Grass* into essayistic prose, flattening the poetic enjambments into paragraph form so that the voice of his poetry merges with that of his essay. Is this merely a stylistic choice on Whitman's part, or is there a direct pathway from poetry-inflected prose—what he calls the 'democratic vista'—to the idea of aesthetic democracy?

2

What is aesthetic democracy? For Whitman, aesthetic democracy is realized in the simultaneity of objective, institutional freedom and the freedom of individual personalities. Institutional freedom is 'sufficient in its scientific aspect, cold as ice,' while that of personalities is 'freedom from all laws or bonds except those of one's own being, control'd by the universal ones.' In Whitman's formula, institutional freedom corresponds with the rational, and personal freedom with the religious. The literary expression of reason is prose, the language of cogency, while that of religion is poetry, the language of indeterminacy. And since aesthetic democracy can only be realized in the simultaneity of objective and personal freedoms, which in turn posits the simultaneity of reason and religion (expressed by prose and poetry respectively), then the literary expression of aesthetic democracy depends on the simultaneous use of poetry and prose. There is, therefore, a direct link between Whitman's choice of literary form and the idea of aesthetic democracy, and this is what he calls the democratic vista.

3

A democratic vista is prose that is pliant to poetry. When prose is pliant to poetry, it means that prose bends to the authority of poetry without giving up its own self-concept. Prose and poetry each have their own manner of dispensing authority. For prose, the dispensation of authority is horizontal, democratic, requiring the reader to use reason to receive the argument. Its authority corresponds with the objective, institutional, and rational elements of democracy. Poetry, on the other hand, delivers authority vertically, in authoritarian fashion, asking the reader to put faith in claims that are pulled out of the air, without a foundation in reason. Poetry's authority corresponds to the individual, personal, and religious elements of democracy. What happens to prose and poetry in the democratic vista is a two-way redistribution of authority. Poetry flattens—democratizes—its authoritarian delivery, while prose lets itself be lifted off the ground of reason. Whitman puts it this way: 'The elevating and ethereal ideas of the unknown and of unreality must be brought forth with authority, as they are legitimate heirs of the known, and of reality...' The absorption of poetry into prose in the democratic vista is Whitman's attempt to create a literary form specifically tailored for the articulation of aesthetic democracy, a literary form which, like its political corollary, straddles 'unreality' (the undisclosed, ideal future of democracy) and 'reality' (democracy's extant objectivity, expressed rationally in its equitable institutions). Prose anticipates its eventual absorption of poetry in the democratic vista, just as America's institutions, according to Whitman, anticipate the education of the people into democratic personalities.

On poetry and prose

1

Poetry and prose are less modes of writing than metaphors for the life of thought. Poetry corresponds to the deep symbolic awakening that happens during childhood; prose, to the recollection of that awakening during adulthood. Poetry is nearer to spontaneous bursts of emotion. It aims to be precocious about its subject. Prose is nearer to the discipline of learning and prefers retrospection. Yet the two are less opposed than related. While corresponding to different modes of cognition, both are clarified through reading. Poetry, when it ages out of spontaneity into self-awareness, inevitably adopts some of the mannerisms of prose; while prose, as it gets honed by study, cannot but learn the limitations of argument. Thus poetry is distinguishable from prose only once it ages into prose, through self-awareness, just as prose stands apart from poetry only after the laws of argument force it to revert to a dependency on symbols. The conclusion is that neither poetry nor prose can come into its own without a middle term of reading. But then what is reading? For poetry, it seems to be a catalyst for symbols to seek the legitimacy of concepts. For prose, reading whittles away the cogency of concepts until their symbolic scaffolding is exposed. Put another way, reading matures the poet and humiliates the prose writer, turning them less toward perfection than toward an appreciation of their respective dilemmas. For the young writer, writing is the fraught labor of hedging the maturation of symbols against the deterioration of concepts—a struggle with the effects of reading on thinking.

2

Proper reading draws the poetic mind toward argument and forces the argumentative mind back toward poetry. There are two ways to approach reading when it is understood this way. The first is the canonical path, along which the reader is faithful that an ordained program of texts will lead the mental struggle between symbolic and conceptual thinking that characterizes adulthood. Canonical reading implies that a collective neuropathway, so to speak, is blazing through the great books, which then has a genetic effect on subsequent thought. The second is the iconoclastic path, which is comparatively less streamlined. Iconoclastic reading is concerned with brains rather than books. It presupposes the universality of mental struggle and contends that because there is no way to reconcile, only negotiate, the division of poetic from prosaic thought, that reading should be improvised in accordance with the desires of readers. Despite this difference of approach, canonical reading is never fully canonical, nor iconoclastic reading fully iconoclastic. Canons, if they recognize history, must be open to new acquisitions, which by virtue of their newness relate iconoclastically toward the old. At the same time iconoclasms, by definition, depend on canons for evaluating the success of their rebellions, and so on some level must admit their conspiracy with authority. Where these two paths converge is their openness to the new. But whereas canons select the new according to old criteria, based on a commitment to temporal continuity, iconoclasms inaugurate the new by severing ties with the old. Logically, then, it would seem that canons bring history along, while iconoclasms leave history behind. And yet the opposite is true. The canonical ideal—proffering the best of the old with the best of the new—collapses in its commitment to continuity. Canons proffer the old at the risk of crystallizing its meaning. When the question of value arises, canonists lean on the grandeur of the representative, rather than the mental struggle it represents, thereby severing it from present concerns. On the other hand, iconoclasts begin right in the middle of history, obsessing over the struggle of reading as it pertains to the present, and in this sense are nearer to understanding the fraught passage of historical (and for that matter, personal) moments. Iconoclastic reading is the beginning of proper reading, yet its dependency on canonical authority cannot be overstated. Though its goal is to break from canonical reading, its success is nevertheless bound to the health of canons.

3

The goal of proper reading is to form the democratic imagination. Proper reading is democratic because it validates the reader's desire to experience the effects that reading has on thinking without having to defer to an unassailable cognitive authority. Yet the desire for firsthand experience is valid only once it attaches itself to its most authoritarian inhibitor; desire earns validation through deferral. What proper reading encourages, then, is not a hope for the eventual reconciliation between canonical and iconoclastic reading, but a desire for humiliation, a longing to be subjugated to the difficulty of thought: of being compelled to hedge between poetry, the maturation of symbols, and prose, the deterioration of concepts. The drive to read originates in this difficulty; the drive to write is how thought struggles with it.

On authority and originality

1

Etymologically, authority and originality share a common aim: The word author comes from the Latin noun *auctor*, which is from the verb *augere*, meaning to promote or originate. To authorize, then, is to have the power of an originator. The desire for originality and the desire for authority are semantically bound. But how can this stand, if authority and originality are also in conflict? It stands because while the two concepts converge in aim, they diverge in origin. Authority begins in circular reasoning, while originality begins in rebellion against that circularity. Authority cannot falter and remain itself. The slightest internal fracture threatens the whole concept. Conversely, originality must fail in order to actualize itself. In rebelling against authority, it does not just risk failure, it wholeheartedly commits to it. Were its rebellion to triumph, originality would merely substitute itself for the extant authority, thereby contradicting its origin. Success is the 'end'—the aim and the demise—of originality.

2

Failure, which is a necessary condition for originality, introduces metaphor to thought. A metaphor is a word that balks at its object of reference. The first sense of the English verb to balk connotes hesitation, a failure to act. The second sense originates from an Old Norse noun, *bálkr*, which means partition. To balk metaphorically is to leave a partition between a word and its object. When a metaphor balks, it corresponds with its object inexactly, half referring to its object's meaning, half to the partition between. The antithesis of metaphor is literality, success. A thought literally pursued demands that a word totally possess its object, without intervention, lest it fail to uphold its standard of success. The distinction between metaphor and literality, therefore, is the distinction between failed and successful thoughts.

3

Metaphor has two ways of balking at objects of reference. The first is through metonym, the substituted name; the second is through pseudonym, the false name. Metaphor mitigates itself in the metonym and indulges itself in the pseudonym. A law of substitution governs metonym, implying that the object of reference still inheres in the word, yet through a veil. Metonym fulfills its responsibility to correspond with its object even as it fails to disclose it wholly. Pseudonym, on the other hand, refuses any responsibility to correspond. It lures metaphor toward total failure by dissociating the word from its object of reference. Metonym is metaphor's proper mode, pseudonym its specious one.

4

Because it is parted from its object, metaphor requires a middle term of translation to make it intelligible. Metonyms are translatable by virtue of being in constant communication with their objects of reference. Pseudonyms, in refusing to correspond with an object, do not assent to translation, preferring to refer ad infinitum to their own penchant for falseness. Translation therefore deals exclusively with metonyms. The goal of translation is to render the partition between a metonym and its object translucent. But why an ideal of translucency and not, for example, transparency? Transparency deceptively promises to render the partition between a metonym and its object invisible (and therefore semantically negligible), whereas translucency proffers but a silhouette of the object. In other words, translation aspires to translucency in order to validate the partial view that metonym offers. If translation goes too far in trying to clarify the object of reference, it forces metonym into the transparency of literality. Then again, if translation neglects the object of reference altogether, it risks total opacity, collapsing the metonym into pseudonym. Conceptually, then, translucency is an ideal of impartiality between transparency and opacity. Yet how could metaphor, whose definitive feature is to be partial to its object, also require impartiality? The only available conclusion is a split one: metaphor must be partial to be translatable, impartial to be valid.

5

A proper metaphor's partiality is predicated on an inexact yet sustained correspondence with its object of reference. This is what makes it translatable. Its impartiality, in turn, is predicated on a simultaneous negation of transparency and opacity, which is what renders the metaphor translucent, valid. The validity of metaphor is proportional to the degree of its impartiality. What is most impartial is likewise most just. A proper metaphor wants justice for its object. Justice validates the partiality of metaphors while upholding the integrity of their objects. An object has integrity insofar as it is bound to a metaphor that fails to disclose it wholly. The failure of metaphors to disclose their objects of reference is both the beginning and the end of their validity: a beginning in that failure is necessary for incompleteness, an end in that the acceptable standard of failure for metaphors is so utterly tenuous as to leave them constantly at risk of saying too much or too little.

6

Metonym, or proper metaphor, is the basic unit of democratic cognition. The word democratic applies specifically to metonym's substitutive character. On the one hand, a metonym is a substitute for the object it names; on the other, a metonym is itself substitutable, in that its failure to disclose its object mortally endangers its validity, necessitating its periodic replacement. Substitutability levels the rank of metonyms such that, once they have established a proper relationship with their objects of reference, no metonym has authority over any other. Insofar as they are antithetical to authority and inclined to fail, metonyms are original. As the basic unit of democratic cognition, metonyms are the link between the concepts of democracy and originality, for it is precisely the democratic element of metonyms—their renunciation of rank, their levelness with every other of their kind —that enables them to be progenitors of original thought.

Spring, Anew

PART ONE

1

Again, anew: again meaning once more, the return of the same; anew meaning once more, in a new and different way. One deepens meaning by repetition, the other by restoration. One advances by iteration, the other by invention. Is one truer than the other? *Again*: time is an intelligible cycle made of mysterious moments. *Anew*: time defers our understanding. *Again*: time apprehends us. *Anew:* time startles us.

2

Perhaps it is not a question of correctness. Perhaps there is a time for one and a time for the other, again and anew, each in its proper moment. Again qualifies autumn, anew spring. The fall after the summer solstice is the first intimation that the seasons are in a holistic cycle, a zero sum of gains and losses of life. Only autumn has this holism in its concept. More than any other moment of the year, the September equinox turns the truth of the whole, carrying the weight of what comes before and after it. The March equinox does something altogether different. Spring appears to restore life out of nothing, anew, as if what was lost during winter could be regenerated in full, and continue being regenerated, life advancing without regard for ends. Where autumn is world-weary and wise, spring is brash and ignorant, separated by summer from the fact of the sun's decline. In the course of this fourfold cycle, spring must forget what comes before it in order to give the impression of having restored life out of nothing. Moreover, it must be blind to what comes after it, so that it can send life into summer without balking at the knowledge that, come autumn, life will fold back on its gains. It is a familiar narrative: *again* goes with autumn and qualifies a deep, reiterated truth; *anew* goes with spring and denotes an advancement of life that is necessarily forgetful, blind.

3

The four-season cycle, turning upon the word *again*, avoids irresolution at the price of sin. Sin happens when a moment of life exceeds the healthful capacity of life's fourfold shape—its 'deific square.' Sin is life in surplus. It thrives between the summer solstice and the autumn equinox, a time when the sun is most generous, yet also starting to decline. After the autumn equinox, beauty, sin's aftermath, begins to manifest sensibly in nature. Beauty is life between sin and absolution, mournfulness revealed in appearance. Mourning is possible insofar as absolution is guaranteed. Autumn mourns sin as it prepares for the cleansing shock of winter. Winter is the guarantor of the fourfold, the fourth corner of the deific square, insuring the significance of the other seasons. It is a revelation of summer's sinful surplus, counterweighing excess with deprivation. In the months between the December solstice and the March equinox, winter erases the sins of the late summer months, absolving life so that it can experience the innocence of restoration, the drawing of the deific square anew, in spring.

4

The four corners of the 'deific square' are ignorance, sin, mourning, and absolution. With absolution comes an unalterable ideal of justice. Life is just when it completes at the end of the cycle. Each year, the deific square encloses the word again, and life completes in a manner that is not random and chaotic, but self-actualized, possessive of meaning. This overall Again, the Again of the fourfold cycle, is greater in scope than the lesser again that belongs to autumn. Autumn arriving again is the repetition of a particular moment in a cycle that is more than the sum of its moments. Yet what about the word anew? Would it be appropriate to speak of the entire cycle recurring Anew, *in a new and different way*? What is new and different is by nature epistemically open, not yet gathered into the known. This is perfectly acceptable for spring, the season of unintelligible beginnings. But the truth of the cycle under Again has to be the overall intelligibility that follows from its mysterious disclosure of a guarantee. If life is insured with a guarantee, then the word Anew has to be excluded from modifying the overall cycle.

The deific square cedes to sin in order to control what might be worse than sin—this unknowable open-endedness of Anew. Sin is the cost of forgetting the possibility that life, in the beginning, could as validly have been proclaimed unfair and futile, as just and worthwhile. This is the danger of the word Anew: when it trespasses beyond its proper moment in spring, it threatens the conceptual integrity of life.

PART TWO

1

The literary form that honors the deific square is the elegy, the mournful ode. The wail of the elegist does not indicate true anguish, but a deep and abiding faith that life is just. Mourning is most painful where faith is strongest. To truly mourn, an elegy must speak with unyielding faith from a dark moment between sin and absolution. The essence of faith is pre-cognitive, committing itself before the mind gets engaged. Faith nominates life as an object worthy of mourning. Life is worthy when it is bound to an ideal of justice that holds without polemic. The first element of justice must be intuitive like faith, of a higher authority, while the second element is cognitive, of a counterweight. What is this higher authority? Etymologically, to wield authority means to be able to originate from nothing, as life does when it restores itself in spring. Authority also has the power of increase, as life increases itself in the spring and summer months. A pure state of authority would demand endless originality and increase, a perennial surplus of life. Yet this surplus would be incompletely just. A second element, a counterweight to authority, is needed to render justice fully. This counterweight brings equanimity—evenness of mind—to the dispensation of authority. Justice is authority counterweighted by even-mindedness, or faith checked retroactively by thought. Yet thought does not check faith in order to undo it, but to make it intelligible. Intelligibility is a yearning for what does not need to be explained. The elegy is the voice of the mind speaking from the frontier of intelligibility, looking back upon ineffable terrain.

2

John Keats' 1819 poem, 'To Autumn,' sets the elegiac precedent for thought mourning faith:

> Season of mists and mellow fruitfulness,
> Close bosom-friend of the maturing sun;
> Conspiring with him how to load and bless
> With fruit the vines that round the thatch-eves run;
> To bend with apples the moss'd cottage-trees,
> And fill all fruit with ripeness to the core;
> To swell the gourd, and plump the hazel shells
> With a sweet kernel; to set the budding more,
> And still more, later flowers for the bees,
> Until they think warm days will never cease,
> For Summer has o'er-brimm'd their clammy cells.

Who hath not seen thee oft amid thy store?
Sometimes whoever seeks abroad may find
Thee sitting careless on a granary floor,
Thy hair soft-lifted by the winnowing wind;
Or on a half-reap'd furrow sound asleep,
Drows'd with the fume of poppies, while thy hook
Spares the next swath and all its twined flowers:
And sometimes like a gleaner thou dost keep
Steady thy laden head across a brook;
Or by a cider-press, with patient look,
Thou watches the last oozings, hours by hours.

Where are the songs of Spring? Ay, where are they?
Think not of them, thou hast thy music too,—
While barred clouds bloom the soft-dying day,
And touch the stubble plains with rosy hue;
Then in a wailful choir the small gnats mourn
Among the river sallows, borne aloft
Or sinking as the light wind lives or dies;
And full-grown lambs loud bleat from hilly bourn;
Hedge-crickets sing; and now with treble soft
The redbreast whistles from a garden-croft;
And gathering swallows twitter in the skies.

Keats' poem speaks from a purgatorial moment between sin and absolution. The poet assigns two responsibilities to autumn. The first is to be handler of summer's overabundance—'Conspiring with [the sun] how to load and bless'; the second is to mourn, through beautiful music, the turning of the fourfold process—'Then in a wailful choir the small gnats mourn...' For Keats, autumn's music is a harmony of fruitfulness and loss. Choirs of gnats, bleating lambs, singing hedge-crickets, whistling redbreasts, twittering swallows, all work in concert to celebrate autumn's 'o'erbrimm'd' abundance, and to lament the turning of the now-declining year.

Autumn's chorus is not the only echo in Keats' ear. In the first line of the last stanza, memory of spring momentarily distracts the poet—'Where are the songs of Spring? Ay, where are they?' This is a curious interjection in an otherwise unbroken ode. Suddenly, autumn's beauty is self-conscious, diminished by a comparison to the other equinox. The comparison feels inappropriate in a poem that purports to enumerate the perfections of the season at hand, not dwell on the traits of other seasons. There seems to be a note of competition in Keats' comparison as well, for the poet finds it necessary to reassure his September muse that its music is equally worthy of notice as spring's. Why would autumn's music need reassurance against the songs of spring, if they did not somehow threaten it? The exclamation, 'Ay, where are they?' tinges the comparison with anguish, as if autumn's orchestral splendor could potentially fall short of spring's brasher, livelier song.

The stakes of the musical competition between autumn and spring are for stewardship over beauty. To steward beauty, according to Keats' own declaration in 'Ode on a Grecian Urn,' is to abide with the sole knowable truth on earth. Thus spring threatens autumn's claim to a truth that appears as mourning and absolution, replacing it with its own idea of truth as forgetfulness and ignorance. The poet's mention of spring is a skillfully suppressed doubt that mourning is truer to life than forgetfulness, and that the elegy is the proper literary form for publishing truth.

The competition between the two equinoxes is part of a darker exploration of the significance of winter, the season standing between the present autumn and the coming spring. Keats dreads these long-suffering months that have the authority to decide whether to judge life mercifully or cruelly. Winter is the one season of the four that 'To Autumn' does not address: summer is 'o'er-brimm'd'; autumn is summer's 'Close bosom-friend'; spring is autumn's musical peer; yet nothing of winter. What is winter's task? Does winter absolve life, as the elegist anticipates, or does it bring him disappointment? Is the task of poetry to fall elegiacally toward winter, as the mourning poet does, or would poetry do better to rise polemically out of winter, renouncing all faith in the completeness of the cycle, marking instead, with every turn of the four, not the word *Again*, but the word *Anew*, the cycle never quite repeating, but reimagining itself, year after year, in a new and different, as yet unknown, way?

3

Winter portends the separation of mind from body. Henry David Thoreau begins the third to last chapter of *Walden*, titled 'The Pond in Winter,' thus:

> After a still winter night I awoke with the impression that some question had been put to me, which I had been endeavoring in vain to answer in my sleep, as what—how—when—where?

Thoreau does not remain beheld to this question for long. After an unstated duration (the inestimable time between the ending of one sentence and the beginning of the next), the question put to him by the still winter night finds easy redress:

> But there was dawning Nature, in whom all creatures live, looking in at my broad windows with serene and satisfied face, and no question on her lips. I awoke to an answered question, to Nature and daylight. The snow lying deep on the earth dotted with young pines, and the very slope of the hill on which my house is placed, seemed to say, Forward! Nature puts no question and answers none which we mortals ask. She has long ago taken her resolution.

What is the actual duration of this winter night and morning, when Thoreau is at first visited by doubt, then purged of it by Nature? Should the above excerpts be taken literally, and the reader assume that Thoreau's anecdote elapses in the course of a single night and morning, Nature handling his question immediately, as soon as he wakes to the sunrise on the windowpane? Or is Thoreau writing summarily here, his anecdote in actuality the accumulation of many restless winter nights and mornings without an answer to his question, the duration lasting an entire season at Walden Pond, or even many entire seasons, as time's passing in Walden is sometimes best interpreted?

Nature's preordained answer is to encourage the author to place his faith in what it provides, pre-cognitively, for him. The question that troubles the mind for a 'night,' Nature waives in an instant. With recourse to Nature's candid wisdom, thought needs little persuasion to revert to faith.

Thoreau is working in an unofficially established tradition of wintertime philosophy. Among his predecessors is René Descartes, who sits down to write his Meditations on First Philosophy after he has put on his winter dressing gown and got the evening fire going. Descartes is longer in doubt than Thoreau. It takes the Frenchman not one, but six consecutive evenings of mental labor to prove the distinction of mind from body, a distinction that is both the cause of his faith—the idea of God comes alive in the mind—and the cause for his doubts—the mind can be tricked by the senses.

On the evening of the first meditation, aptly titled 'Concerning Those Things That Can Be Called into

Doubt,' Descartes, like Thoreau, is troubled by his dreams:

> This [not doubting my senses] would all be well and good, were I not a man who is accustomed to sleeping at night, and to experiencing in my dreams the very same things, or now and then even less plausible ones, as [...] insane people do when they are awake. How often does my evening slumber persuade me of such ordinary things as these: that I am here, clothed in my dressing gown, seated next to the fireplace—when in fact I am lying undressed in bed!

As he studies the sensory deceptions of dreams, Descartes takes his first step toward parting mind from body, just as Thoreau's dream parted mind from Nature before he awoke to his question answered. Something about dreaming on a winter's night brings both thinkers to the abyss of intellectual crisis, without quite throwing them in. Each describes a dangerous moment in cognitive life when the mind, in dreamy solipsism, puts a question to Nature or to God, loitering in unanswered suspense, parted by a cognitive wound from the intuitions of faith.

By morning, however, both Thoreau and Descartes get their answers, and become men of faith, again. Each finds his question answered by an infinite, restorative presence, the one calling it 'Nature,' the other 'God.' Yet it is precisely the perfection of the infinite that separates the human mind from it. Perfection causes, then alleviates, the mind's sufferings. When a thinker chooses to abide with an infinite, she implicitly assents to cognitive crisis—that precarious moment of delay when her question has been put, and no answer has been given.

What if—Nature and God forbid it—this delay was to continue elapsing open-endedly, and the questioner had to go on with her life, dispossessed of an answer? What if Nature and God struggled alongside the questioner, and at the end of the long winter, did not absolve the mind of its doubts, but let spring begin, Anew, before the turning of the four was complete?

Apart from justice for the mind, there is tragedy.

4

Tragedy occurs when the inquiring mind asks a question and receives no answer. Tragedy is foremost a cognitive experience, since the mind must first have formed an intelligent question in order for an answer to be missed. Such a dispossession is a deferral of absolution. Absolution defers when the mind falls out of pace with the rest of life and fails to rejoin it. Freezing is the physical expression of the mind falling out of pace. Ice provokes contemplation. When the earth freezes during winter, and the atoms of life are stalled, the mind discovers its own unceasing motion, and begins to doubt the validity of that which is not perennial. Upon this discovery, the mind parts itself from the rest of life in order to steel itself against the stillness surrounding it. This parting is enacted through a question that thought puts to faith. When an answer is not received instantaneously, by way of an extant higher authority, the question has the effect of leveling the questioner. The first sense of *to level* is to destroy, to raze to the ground. The mind deprived of truth is masochistic. It does violence against itself by questioning the intimations of faith. And yet the second sense of *to level* is to bring to balance. The masochistic mind may be violent, but it is also its own authorizer, subordinate to none. It is therefore guilty before none and need not repent for having doubted. Insofar as it is unrepentant, the mind is indifferent to the pull of higher authorities. This indifference nudges the mind to strive for impartiality in judgment. What seeks impartiality seeks justice also. The leveling effect of dispossession, therefore, is an inverted articulation of justice, originating in the autonomy of the mind. What is level, indifferent, and autonomous is insofar democratic. Winter's revelation of cognitive motion is a democratic revelation of justice out of dispossession. The mind dispossessed of an answer must deduce epistemic authority horizontally, of itself, rather than vertically, of an infinite and incomprehensible other. It follows that the democratic ideal is of dispossession, not of absolution. Democracy is borne from prolonged mental winters that conclude incompletely, the main questions left unanswered. Yet the democratic winter does not prove the mind's resilience so much as the mind's enfeeblement under winter's thumb. Winters without absolution damage the mind permanently, wounding it against life.

PART THREE

1

The literary mode of tragedy is the polemic. The polemicist is on the one hand a complainant, on the other hand, an autodidact. As complainant, the polemicist laments having to inherit thought after it has parted ways with faith. Her complaint is that the life of the mind is retrograde, impossibly inclined toward a faith it never knew and, now that the two have been divided, can no longer hope to possess. The faithless are disconsolate. While the elegist mourns past sins committed, the polemicist keens for lack of opportunity. Untouched by sin, the complainant has a totally inverted sense of what a life freely lived might be. Whereas the freedom of the elegist is to mold thought in the image of faith, kneeling at winter's forgiving altar, the freedom of the polemicist, since she has been allocated nothing, is to cognitively self-determine her own ends, pledging allegiance to the coming spring. As her freedom is concerned, the polemicist is not only a complainant, but also an autodidact, and the antithesis of absolution is not only dispossession, but also education. Those from whom mercy is withheld are let to teach themselves. Coddled by no authority, the way of their education is necessarily negative, ironic. An ironic education unfolds in two phases. The first phase is exposure to the crisis of incompletion. Dispossession teaches what it is like to be guaranteed nothing; out of nothing, irony quickens in the mind. The second phase of an ironic education is *humiliation*—from the Latin *humus*, ground—which connotes a leveling to the ground. A sound polemic is a complaint that levels its object in both a destructive and a democratic sense. Unlike the elegy, which seeks to apprehend and honor justice, the polemic is an ironic simulation of faith, justice out of nothing, seeking with every aggrieved word to invoke a new order and to forget its complaint against life.

2

The classic polemic in American letters is Ralph Ellison's 1952 novel, *Invisible Man*. The novel's protagonist, the Invisible Man, is a young, disillusioned black man speaking from 'hibernation,' making his metaphorical social invisibility literal by withdrawing into the underground of Manhattan, where he can think his own thoughts without feeling compelled to placate the undemocratic society that torments him above ground. In this subterranean schoolhouse of sorts, he teaches himself ironies that bring his existence back to sufferable terms. The goal of his ironic education is at once noble and narcissistic. He will tell his own life story, down to the last humiliating detail, because he believes his life important enough to make it a problem for others to consider.

With *Invisible Man*, Ellison discovers two essential elements of the tragic conception of life. The first is that the terms of dispossession become, perversely, the terms of freedom. Above ground, the Invisible Man's life was made miserable by his compulsion, at once conscious and unconscious, to placate others' expectations of a black person's comportment in public life. To play this placating role well, he had to suppress the originality of his own intelligence, lest he give the impression of being a misfit or a rabble-rouser. When he goes underground, the Invisible Man rediscovers the cause of his aboveground immiseration—'the mind, *the mind*'—and from this personal cognitive misery, creates a polemic that focuses on the problems of humanism and democracy more generally, as if to imply that the individual life, *his* life, touches upon universal themes, the bare unit substituting for the whole.

The Invisible Man recycles his dispossession as privilege by offering up his life as a metonym. Yet by no means is metonymy a state of freedom without responsibility. Insofar as the unit claims to name the universal, the former becomes disproportionately responsible to the latter. In a deeply unfair sense, the dispossessed person is the most cognitively burdened, much more so than those whose intuitions prove them correct on a regular basis. Abandoned to the mind, it is the disconsolate who end up having to teach the faithful that the tragic sense of life is the sole sufferable one, and, moreover, the sole *defensible* one, once the truth of dispossession has been proved. The Epilogue to

Invisible Man defends a tragic conception of democracy on the presumption that without tragedy, politics, like the narrator's metonymic life, would be utterly without aspirations. If 'humanity is won by continuing to play in face of certain defeat,' then humanity should not belong to those unmindful of tragedy. Blind faith, according to the narrator, does not encourage ongoing humanization and democratization. Despondency, however, does.

The Invisible Man's last words are carefully chosen. 'Who knows'—he asks—'but that, on the lower frequencies, I speak for you?' His polemic concludes not with an answer but with a new unanswerable question, which he puts to his reader from the vantage point of freedom. The Invisible Man's freedom is his dispossession, recycled as privilege. His privilege is that he can make a metonym of his tragic life, naming the democratic universal with the personal. Part of this privilege is putting questions to his peers that upset their faith in the basic justice of public, not to mention spiritual, life. 'There's a stench in the air,' he writes, 'which, from this distance underground, might be the smell either of death or of spring—I hope spring.' Which will it be, he asks from below—death or spring, Anew?

3

Is a polemic beautiful like an elegy? If so, the definition of beauty would have to be reconstructed as the appearance in the sensible world of dispossession, recycled as privilege.

Beauty would have to reveal a form of freedom that self-determines out of nothing. Such counterintuitive thinking would have to be hedged retroactively against intuition. The polemic, however, is faithless and mistrusting of intuitions. Thus the polemicist has no choice but to argue against the apparent indisputability of intuitively beautiful appearances. Beauty in its polemical form has to be screened by thought before it can appear in the world. Thought does not screen beauty to control it, but to cognize it, and to pass a judgment on it. A judgment is nothing more than a claim supported by reasons. Beauty must be defended with reasons, lest it be degraded to a fetish. The word fetish recalls the Latin word *facticius*, which in English became factitious, 'artificially made.' Intuition makes beauty a fetish by failing to come to its defense. Consequently, the most intuitive is not the truest to beauty, but the most given over to artifice. Whereas what follows from judgment, while counterintuitive, labors toward the end of letting beauty be. A sound judgment proves that the beautiful must be *cognitively earned* before it can ever become common sense. Letting beauty be is a skill acquired through an aesthetic education of the mind.

4

An aesthetic education trains the mind to earn beauty counterintuitively. The hallmark of an aesthetic education is the ability to discern between an elegy and a polemic—between art that follows an eloquent intuition of beauty, and art that makes a laborious judgment of it. The distinction is less substantial than temporal. An elegy apprehends beauty in the instant; a polemic finds beauty in delay. The instant offers a straightforward edict; the delay, an education in cunning. An aesthetic education persuades the mind by cunning. The word cunning originates from an Old Norse noun, *kunnandi*, which means knowledge. In Middle English, *kunnandi* became *can*, connoting erudition. Over time, as *can* became *cunning*, the word evolved to connote deceit. Aesthetic education is analogous to the transformation of *can*, erudition, into *cunning*, deceit. The mind is ingenious to the degree it is capable of deceiving itself with its own judgments. Far from being a deliberate recollection of what is already known, aesthetic education is willful self-deception in judgment, cunning applied against intuition, to no known end.

PART FOUR

1

Spring, Anew. Over Riverside Park, the afternoon sky glares gunmetal, a distinctively mid-March color that hints it is neither winter anymore, nor spring quite yet. The sycamore and the sky are of one hue, as if the tree were the barely concealed skeleton of the earth, holding the Overall in place. Though not yet green, cautious leaf-buds are forming along the sycamore's branches, and its roots, after months of dormancy, are quivering in the ground. By all appearances, the tree is on the cusp of resurgence. And yet it would be just as valid to say that the sycamore still bears a look of wintry ruin, scarred bone-deep by the cold. The tree's bareness divides it from its surroundings, its profile not conforming with the mid-March colorscape, but negating any relation to it at all. The sycamore's simultaneous conformism and distinctiveness are most apparent on days like today, just before the March equinox, before the air has gotten consistently warm and spring advanced beyond regress. In a few weeks' time, the sycamore's cautious leaf-buds will be modest green leaves, neither in obvious conformism, nor in notable contrast, with the colors around them. A trace of winter will inhere in the greening body, for while it does have a hardier look once its leaves come in, in fact its foliage spreads pretty sparsely along the branch, the robust trunk uncrowded by the bloom, so that even at the height of its June health, the sycamore will have failed to thaw its winter skeleton back to life.

*

In the periodic silences that settle over East River Park, the only audible sound from the quay is that of the ice floes colliding and cracking as they drift with the slow, but quickening, current. As the larger floes melt, they break into smaller chunks that, haphazardly drifting, ram against each other, collecting into random, angular masses that float together for a few minutes or hours before disassembling downriver. These temporary floating sculptures are best viewed at twilight, when the electric reflection of Manhattan's Lower East Side beams down to the river, hitting the sculptures at oblique angles, so that blue shadows form on the broad-faced floes, and the silhouettes of the sculptures shimmer yellow with light. Often, two sculptures will drift ashore at the same time and pin each other against the quay, stalling there, warming under the light, until one of them melts free and dissolves into partial shadow. This process will continue for a few more days until every floe rejoins the current, at which point Manhattan's electric reflection will show unobstructed on the water. Yet a certain effect will have been lost in the change. Twilit evenings will no longer witness the yellow shimmer of the ice sculptures as they stall against the quay. Once the East River's current warms to speed, the reflections of Manhattan's towers will become monotonous mirages on its brackish surface, fodder for postcard kitsch, reiterated in every drop of water that passes through their undiscriminating light.

2

Easter arrives just as the first golden leaves are breaking on the willows that border the creek on the west side of town. The sagging boughs crimp the sunrise in pale threads, weaving a canopy of leaves and light above the creek. Up the hill, the streets are packed with solemn traffic, mostly young families and elderly people observing the Easter holiday, driving or walking to nine a.m. worship. Many in the throng look underrested, particularly the mothers with small children, yet many, if not most, of the elderly, look positively placid and ready to spend the next hour fishing for souls in the name of the resurrected Christ. Besides the churches, the town's other locus of activity is down the hill, at the creek bordered by willows. A handful of sturdy men toting fishing tackle and beverage coolers have distributed themselves evenly along the banks, performing their Sunday sacrament with a reverence to rival that of the Christians. And were it not for the fact that it is Easter morning, and were it not for the near-uniform goatees framing the studied frowns on the men's faces, and were it not for the ethic of silence that pervades their maritime ritual, these men might, as a group, pass for an accidental fraternity of free-thinkers, united by their abstention from rituals that complicate Man's communion with Nature. But that is not quite how they appear. While humble of presentation, these men look more like a fraternal order than a ragtag cadre. The gender exclusivity of the group, while not inherently sexist, betrays a preference for organization over spontaneity. Moreover, these men do not appear to be seeking total solitude, otherwise they would not be fishing in the public stream. They are here to see their fellows, to be in a place where two or more are gathered in the name of the resurrected spring. They are fishing for fish, while their neighbors at the churches go fishing for men. The difference between fishers of fish and fishers of men is one of quantity, rather than quality. After many Easter mornings of contemplation, these men have no additional questions to put to the stream. They know just as well as the believer what it means to be saved.

*

The Moravian Christians who came to America were humble before God and before one another and so marked their graves with plain stones that laid flat upon the ground. In a Moravian cemetery, there are no monuments or private mausoleums. Every stone is identical in size and shape, just as every individual soul is of equal measure on God's just scale. Easter morning witnesses an annual demonstration of this principle, as a few of the town's remaining Moravian descendants gather at the old cemetery for the tradition of placing flowers on the graves of children. The tradition has a profoundly democratic as well as a religious feeling. Even the gravestones of stillborn infants, who never lived an hour outside their mothers' wombs, are lavished with lilacs, their souls weighed equally with the rest.

The lilacs left on the stones are the sole adornments in a burial ground that is notable for its perfect symmetry and humble plainness. The cemetery is exactly a square city block in area, divided by two walking paths that bisect each other in the shape of the cross. The four sides are bordered by a prudent black fence that has no main entrance, but which provides two cater-cornered gates that are not really gates, merely gaps in the fence-line, three feet in width, at the northeast and southwest corners of the grounds.

Judging solely by the design of their cemeteries, the Moravians might have been a sect that imagined God had arranged life on a divine grid, a deific square within whose enclosure each individual was a countable unit of the infinite. Their uniform gravestones were their method of keeping the tally as they waited for God to unburden them of trying in vain to understand His divine calculus. Identification with God was the source of the Moravians' mathematical identicalness to one another. Their self-leveling imitated a Being that enumerated individuals as vulgar integers long before He assigned them proper names.

But until the faithful are unburdened of the task of counting to infinity, their tallying, however great, will never be enough. Inevitably, a democracy of the faithful will feel the need to flatten itself under the burden of God's innumerable mercies. Perhaps this is why, apart from the inherent historical value of the tradition, the descendents of the Moravians continue attending to infants who died in 1863, 1877, 1894, 1903. Perhaps if these children had survived and lived full lives, the tally might have filled the grid, or at least have gotten further along, and the heaviness of identicalness—the dead weight of a stone—might have been lifted from their minds, allowing them to imagine a life beyond piety.

After every child's stone has been decorated with lilacs, the attendants gather in the center of the cemetery for a closing prayer. The ceremony ends with a silent single-file procession that exits through the gate at the southwest corner of the cemetery, dispersing onto the campus of the adjacent Central Moravian Church, where, out of the open doors of the sanctuary, the pipe organ booms the first note of the opening choral, and the Easter worship hour commences.

3

Wallace Stevens' poem, 'Meditation Celestial & Terrestrial,' concerns the difficulty of understanding the passage from winter to summer.

It might be re-titled, in symmetry with John Keats, 'To Spring':

The wild warblers are warbling in the jungle
Of life and spring and of the lustrous
inundations,
Flood on flood, of our returning sun.

Day after day, throughout the winter,
We hardened ourselves to live by bluest reason
In a world of wind and frost,

And by will, unshaken and florid
In mornings of angular ice,
That passed beyond us through the narrow sky.

> But what are radiant reason and radiant will
> To warblings early in the hilarious trees
> Of summer, the drunken mother?

As in Keats' 'To Autumn,' Stevens' poem devolves upon a comparative question. Keats' question—'Where are the songs of Spring? Ay, where are they?'—compares the beauty of the two equinoxes from a moment between sin and absolution. Stevens' question—'What is radiant reason to drunken summer?'—compares the authority of the two solstices during the final forgetful weeks of spring. A rephrasing of Stevens' question to match Keats' might be: have we begun anew out of absolution or dispossession?

The lightness of phrasing is what makes the question so effective. It can be taken in several directions at once. One valid take is that the poet's question is meant to be rhetorical, and by comparing the cognitive hardships of winter to the drunken hilarities of summer, he means to endorse indolence ahead of industry. Another, equally valid, interpretation is that the form of the question is meant to inspire a counterintuitive reading, one that accounts for the whole poem instead of isolating a single moment. The counterintuitive reading accepts the question at face value—but what is winter to summer?—and patiently reviews the evidence. Winter is 'will, unshaken and florid' compared to 'wild warblers.' It is 'bluest reason' compared to 'hilarious trees.' It is 'radiant will compared to the 'drunken mother.' Juxtaposing these associations, is one indisputably better than the other? Is a 'lustrous inundation,' for some inarguable reason, very preferable to 'angular ice,' even if the former inebriates the mind, while the latter invigorates it?

In a delayed reading, Stevens' question, like Keats', retains its comparative openness. But, unlike Keats, Stevens' poetic levity disguises an underlying seriousness, suggesting that this author, where spring is concerned, prefers cunning to mournfulness.

4

Can the smell of grass be cunning? It depends where the grass grows.

In the uptown Manhattan neighborhood of Washington Heights, a steep declivity that overlooks the Hudson River is home to Trinity Cemetery, the only active cemetery left in Manhattan. Since the cemetery ran out of pre-orderable burial space years ago, the management has been selling aboveground crypts that are located in a public mausoleum at the foot of the hill. The crypts are expensive, inaccessible to the majority of the 60,000 people who die in New York City every year.

Like most solutions to Manhattan's social problems, the mathematics of burying the dead is cold as ice: no space, no new plots. Or, now that the aboveground crypt is an option at Trinity: no money, no plots. Even the dead get gentrified in New York.

But supposing class issues were not in play, and the housing crisis of the dead were simply an issue of geography, there would still be too little ground and too many people. This definition of the problem casts the extravagant private crypts and towering monuments-to-self of bygone Astors and Hamiltons in a troubling light. Wealthy nineteenth-century Manhattanites seem to have had no foresight at all when it came to constructing their final resting places. They built too big, too early. Didn't they ever stop to think about those who were to follow them in death, legions of unborn New Yorkers who will have loved the city just as much as they loved it, and who will have wished, just as they wished, to make an eternal home in it?

Of course they didn't think about that—just look at the graves. Yet the presence of swanky stones amid spatial scarcity is no longer the important thing to notice about Trinity Cemetery, not now that the solution to the problem—aboveground crypts—follows the same free-market, 'pay to decay' logic of New York's nineteenth-century elite. Nowadays, what is more compelling than the literal class politics of burial, or even the fantastical art on some of the older monuments, is the smell of the grass that grows upon the graves. Near the 154th Street summit, there is a secluded knoll that by early May starts to give off a humid, vinegary scent not unlike the scent of human perspiration on cotton clothing. The grass sweats. It sweats on the graves of Trinity Cemetery just as it would sweat on the dandelions of Ohio hillsides, or on the feet of palm trees in rural Florida. The smell of the sweating grass is dewy and warm, with a bite of tart that makes it a taste as well.

'And if nothing more,' the Invisible Man writes from underground, 'invisibility has taught my nose to classify the stenches of death.'

It is early May, the air is balmy, the grass is sweating on the knoll. What is there to disqualify this as one among the many 'stenches of death'?

Indeed, what keeps the nose from sneaking a whiff of death on a sunny noon in May? And what keeps the mind from judging afterward: This is the smell of spring, Anew.

MICHAEL SKELTON
▇ Hamilton Avenue, Apt. ▇
Cincinnati, OH ▇

To Whom It May Concern:

I am writing to apply for the Fall 2014 opening for Liberal Arts—Adjunct Instructor, as listed on the ▇ web site. With a disciplinary background in comparative literature, philosophy, and aesthetics, combined with several years' experience teaching writing at the university level, I feel strongly that I could offer ▇ students a broad survey of the philosophical ideas that have influenced artists over the centuries, as well as a challenging introduction to college-level oral communication and writing.

I received my graduate disciplinary training in Comparative Literature at ▇ University. I chose the discipline because it required me to hedge at all times between literature and philosophy, while introducing me to a range of languages, texts, and art histories. My thesis synthesized the cross-disciplinary theoretical work I was encouraged to do. I wrote on the pervasiveness of irony in texts from the early period of modern Chinese literature, relating the 'ironic turn' in Chinese fiction, which occurred during a moment of unprecedented contact with the modern Western canon, to philosopher Soren Kierkegaard's idea that 'ironists' arise at historic moments of cultural and epistemological transformation.

The lessons from my graduate work have carried into my teaching, where I try to teach cross-disciplinary methods of inquiry. I frequently use film as an entryway to historical topics, and I assign readings that challenge my students to look for parallel trends in mass culture and politics. Pedagogically, my first priority is to teach rigorous thinking; then I coach the art of writing. This is how I was taught to write by my best professors, and I have come to believe it is the ideal way.

I'll conclude on a personal note. I have been eagerly awaiting an opportunity to teach the books and ideas I love in so rich an intellectual environment. I would relish the opportunity to teach philosophy to young artists at such a pivotal moment in their creative development. Thank you for considering my application.

Sincerely,
Michael Skelton

Early attempt to define a democratic radicalism

Concomitantly with our digital atemporality comes a political atemporality that negates the historical struggle it took to achieve our present ideals. Today, the propaganda of efficiency politics disguises the ongoing counter-revolution against all ideologies that demand economic equality alongside equality before the law. Technological solutionism reflects the algorithmic imaginations that contrive it. Global commercialism, no matter the trader's language, is global monolingualism. Confronting this situation, the democratic radical has necessarily had to learn to coexist with visions of the world that are fundamentally undemocratic. In one sense this is liberating for her, in that she and her fellows are no longer beholden to naive dreams of utopian futures, and are now looking to their short-term possibilities with jaded eyes. Yet there is also an enslavement in this kind of resignation, since it requires of democrats (who have always searched despairingly for the meaning of justice in *history*) to adjust their goals in accordance with a capitalist society that strives to subjugate the majority to the whims of finance. 'Democracy' in the twenty-first century does not name an achievable political reality so much as an unrelenting struggle against these political (and intellectual) subjugations, a struggle that no serious democrat believes can be completely won. And while this may be a more realistic program than that put forward by past idealists, this realism appears at the same time that the New Technocrats are promising such fantastical achievements as the technological amelioration of global poverty—the globalization, in other words, of a *de-politicized* capitalistic lifestyle that provides everything but an alternative. Nowhere is there talk of re-instantiating what Walt Whitman once called democratic 'prudence'—the publicly shared conviction that 'he who never peril'd his life, but retains it to old age/in riches and ease, has probably achiev'd/ nothing for himself worth mentioning.'

Notebook entry from May Day, 2012

May 1, 2012, 11PM: a day of conspiracy between politics and nature. Today Occupy Wall Street held demonstrations in most of the public parks in Manhattan and Brooklyn. From the moment I left my apartment in the morning, to when I returned in the evening, I felt I was being stalked by every good and evil intention in the world, my body pushed along by a rogue wind. It was the finest weather I had seen in New York City in months. The city's conscience seemed to be stirring out of its torpid winter sleep at last. I saw thousands of seagulls flocking up the Hudson from New York Harbor, forming a wall of white plumage from Battery Park to Chelsea. The trees in Madison Square exploded—overnight, it seemed—with pink and lavender blossoms, the second wave of flowers in as many weeks. New Yorkers of every imaginable costume turned out for the rallies in Wall Street, Washington Square, Central Park. It was one of those days when the whole island of Manhattan, above and below ground, agreed, as if by silent contract, to gather its millions of incommensurable fragments into a single critical mass, which, though it lacked a central nucleus, articulated, nevertheless, the immensity of its cohesion.

Untenable

Our institutions of Love resemble always
the brutal pieties that propel us toward them;
whereas, duty to none in particular
draws us nearer to our center of mass,
and forgoing that Love
magnifies the as real beloveds
whom we keep at arms' length.

A rising, objectless love
would start from the presumption
that the untenable cognitive utopia
could be as populous as the Earth:
that every last idiolect
babbling in Brussels' amphitheaters
could chant the constitution
of a single, diachronic vision.

two **MYSTICISM**

Locked in that strength we stay and stay
And cannot go away
For You have given us our liberty.

Imprisoned in the fortunes of your adamant
We can no longer move, for we are free.

—Thomas Merton, 'Freedom as Experience

At Trappists, Kentucky

1

The silence at Our Lady of Gethsemani cannot rightly be called an absence of speech. A Cistercian monk's private hours are full of self-dialogue and sung prayers, and his social hours are fluent in a rich nonverbal language that develops continuously out of the group's abstention from the spoken word. The communal language of the abbey depends heavily on indirect gestures—footfalls calling to each other from opposite ends of a walkway, garden spades conversing in the dirt; as well as direct gestures—a nod of acknowledgment at the work table; a shared laugh in church that never breaks the lips. Some of the older monks burp and fart with such impunity during the lunch hour that an unsuspecting retreatant could easily mistake their humble dining room for a Spartan mess hall. This communal language cannot but have a creature-likeness to it; the Order is like a murder of crows hungrily encircling the same tree. Their goal in not speaking is not to simplify the meanings of words, but to exploit the multitude of pre-linguistic signs that underwrite them. What does get spoken aloud—the reformed liturgy—is repeated so inexhaustibly that the repetition itself becomes a wordless gesture, the ancient psalms collapsing into unutterable groans of faith.

2

The silence at Gethsemani is better thought of as the voiceless presence of duration. Time is all that passes at the abbey, and all happenings there have a proper time. Trappism is a mode of being that dedicates itself exclusively to purposive action. Every moment of the monk's day is saturated with meaning; meaningless action is the only mortal sin he confronts. The young man who enters the Order does so believing that he is turning his mind upon divine objects alone. He supposes that by silencing his own inner monologue, he gains access to still quieter voices—the voices of nature and time, the voice of God. He claims to hear the very sunrise in the eastern sky, and he pauses when the native birds wake the hushed halls of the abbey with their featherlight hymns of joy. He believes that taking the eucharist in silence magnifies the words of Christ in his heart, and he prays the liturgy, over and over, that he might one day listen louder than he chants.

3

Contemplation, study, prayer: these are the names he assigns to his focus on the silent Word. Yet it is precisely the opposite of focus that the monk attains through the sacraments. For if what he seeks in the monastic life is God's perfect wisdom, then his actions must be for the purpose of receiving revelation. Revelation, however, is less a matter of focus than of distraction. When God imparts a new wisdom, He distracts the recipient from what he previously knew so that it does not hinder his perception of the new. Revelation is God's way of setting into motion a mind that has grown inert with repetition. The monk's knowledge is imperfect, and with each sacramental action, he confesses his lack of understanding to God. Thus the liturgy does not teach the initiate divine wisdom so much as it encourages him to study his ignorance. The Cistercian focuses himself in order to be ready for the moment when God draws his mind away from the plain words of the psalms toward the pre-lingual chants of truth. Only upon receiving this wisdom does the monk break the silence of his days with a moan of agony that signals to God that divine education is taking place.

4

The silence at Gethsemani is an attunement to the duration in which God discloses His voiceless Word. It is the very temporality of wisdom, cancelling the self at the moment in which self-knowledge is attained. The Cistercian creates something other than himself in his repetition of the sacraments. He renounces choice and passion in favor of a liberty that prohibits him from moving from his assigned place in the order of things. Hence he is self-centered only inasmuch as he centers himself in prayer, and he knows himself only as well as he is conscious of his ignorance. The Cistercians are an *order* precisely because it would be impossible to sustain their method of revelation in social isolation. The solitary collective is a buoy in a dark sea of unknowing upon which the faithful are blown and tossed by a divine fury that never relents.

5

This life of silence resolves in a state of motionlessness: *We can no longer move, for we are free*. The monk's lack of movement is first of all physical. The monastery is a world in miniature, and life there is such that all initiates must worship in one church, work in one garden, and walk in one wood that extends for a limited number of acres. Possibilities are less tangible than determinations—and this goes for social life as well. Among the Cistercians, there is no conception of upward or downward mobility, for the simple reason that there is nowhere for an individual to rise or fall in the Order. Identities physical and social are affixed upon arrival and do not change except when it is necessary to redistribute roles of equal value. There is a nominal system of rank within the earthly church that has no bearing in the eternal one. No one leaves the little acreage in Kentucky that God has provided him. No one stoops so low as to climb the corporate ladder of Heaven.

6

Bound to the monastery as if it were the whole Earth, the Order is like a planet in orbit, whirling on an elliptical course that is bound to God's Son by a mysterious gravity. At Gethsemani, the experience of liberty is indistinguishable from the experience of coercion. Desire yields to duty, yet the fulfillment of duty brings a satisfaction that stokes the flame of desire anew, reforming it into the will to yield. The monk thrown into this orbit trusts God's physic as much as he trusts Newton's law. With each renewed act of obedience, he reduces the mass of his own being, plunging himself deeper and deeper into the starry concentricities that pull him closer to his Creator.

7

The monk's hankering for grace originates in the pain that he experiences during his contemplations. Accounting for God is like trying to tally an empty magnitude. It is a presence so permeating and immaterial that it can only be felt as a lack. Revelation is one more mode of suffering through which the feeling of God's absence gets compounded within the self. For to be filled with God is the same as being bankrupted by Him. The education of the contemplative must be understood not as a steady ascent toward godly wisdom, but as a downward spiral into an earthly hell where consolation is scarce. God's grace is the gravity that coerces the recipient out of a state of ignorance about his ignorance into a state of self-conscious deficiency. It is a force of pure terror which the monk cannot resist without giving himself up to total spiritual entropy. *May my bones burn and ravens eat my flesh if I forget thee, contemplation!* Such histrionic outbursts articulate the experience of God's grace more exactly than any ode to joy.

On the mystical and the secular

1

As long as the infinite remains estranged from the finite, so, too, will our approach of divine knowledge be equivalent to the experience of earthly suffering. Catholic mysticism in particular emphasizes suffering as the basis of spiritual education. That suffering is necessary for receiving eternal wisdom is one of its foregone conclusions, given that Christian dogma yields all worthwhile knowing to the infinite and consigns human reasoning to the finite. The consequence of this is that all positively acquired knowledge—knowledge begotten by reason—holds the status of ignorance next to divine knowledge. And because divine knowledge cannot be gained by positive reason, it must disclose itself by a negative method, a method not of cumulative scientific inquiry, but of earnest self-surrender and self-diminishment—what the Catholic mystics variously call suffering, contemplation, supplicative prayer. The trouble with these self-effacing acts of faith is that they never fully distinguish themselves from the one act of bad faith. The originary sin of humanity is not that we betrayed God's sacred ordinance, but that we were born finite, and can never know what God knows as long as earth remains our home. It follows that suffering does not achieve divine wisdom so much as a privileged body of earthly truisms. It reduces the experience of humanity to the experience of ignorance, and in this sense, acknowledges in advance that it will never gain what it seeks. The goal of mystical practice must therefore be the attainment of some kind of self-conscious ignorance. Abiding in this self-consciousness for the duration of an earthly life is what the mystics have traditionally called suffering. The mystic suffers because she experiences knowledge as an indefinite magnitude, rather than as an intelligible body with clear outer dimensions. She carries with her at all times the sense, not unlike a child's, of being totally exposed to uncertainty, with no hope of being rescued from it. Her contradictory desire to heave her entire being into this uncertainty is the fountain of all her misery on earth.

2

The difference between mysticism and secularism is not as great as has been supposed by either side. As a knowledge practice, the mystical has as much in common with the secular as it does with the sacred. This is because the absolute renunciation of God—the secular vow—accomplishes the same thing as the absolute acceptance of God—the sacred vow. Both arrive at the admission that the infinite has flown from the finite; both contemplate the fundamental imperfectability of human knowledge. Where they diverge is in their orientation to the infinite. The secular turns away from the infinite in her avoidance of self-conscious suffering. She suspects that her renunciation of the infinite has not destroyed her consciousness of it, and yet she argues, against the mystic, that there is a qualitative difference between the form of mathematical infinity and the form of God. Mathematical infinity can be manipulated for the ends of human reason, the secular argues, whereas God cannot be manipulated whatsoever for human ends. She is not incorrect. Her mistake is in supposing that the utility of mathematical infinity will alleviate her anxiety about its indefinite extension. All she would have to do unclose the infinite is to think back on herself as a child, when she tried, as every curious child tries, to count to infinity from one, only to grow bored or exhausted with the task. The utility of mathematical infinity is therefore nothing more than a strategic repression of its potential uselessness. The boredom of the child becomes the amnesia of the adult; the secular suffers without remembering that she suffers. And she had better not remember it: otherwise, she might admit that her life is being devoured by an indefiniteness that carries no meaning within the limits of reason alone.

3

It might be asserted that the difference *in experience* between the secular and the mystic is analogous to that between horror and terror. Both undergo fear and intimidation, both endure emotional distress and suffering, but only secular horror carries within it that element of disgust which transforms the feeling of dread into the feeling of revulsion. Here again it is a question of orientation. The one who is terrified, the mystic, turns toward the empty magnitude she calls her God and trembles out of reverence and respect as well as a keen sense of personal inadequacy before the infinite. This holy terror humiliates and edifies her at once. In courting annihilation, the mystic enters her doomed vocation in prayer. The one horrified, the secular, on the other hand, turns toward the superabundant earth, the finite, haunted by the ghost of an infinite long ago buried in her consciousness. The assurance that she is fully adequate to this degraded and deprived world that she confronts daily; moreover, the assurance that she deserves by virtue of her finitude to perish in it without consequence; and finally, the assurance that she will never transcend the earth, but will instead spend the duration of her existence disciplining her imagination to move within the dimensions of her planetary prison, are thoughts so repugnant to her that she will likely wait to entertain them until she is on her way out of this life.

4

Neither mysticism nor secularism can claim more truth-value than the other. While it is true that mysticism is more honest than secularism in acknowledging the pervasiveness of earthly suffering, it would be equally valid to assert that secularism is more honest than mysticism in its total embrace of the world. Neither system recognizes the fundamental truth-claim of the other. Mysticism rejects human reason in favor of an indefinite, divine knowledge that can never be disclosed on earth. Secularism rejects self-conscious ignorance on the grounds that it denies the certainty that can be had within the bounds laid out by human reason. But there is another dimension to the question that is just as important to consider when judging the comparative validity of faith and reason. Consider the respective homes of the mystic versus the secular. Whether at the monastery, at the corporate place of worship, or in solitary retreat, the mystic, in a sense, always occupies *terra aliena*. It should be pointed out, however, that the mystic, and not the land, is the foreign entity, for just as the infinite is a guest within the bounds of human consciousness, so the mystic is a guest upon the land inhabited by unredeemed humanity. Modern mystical traditions have supplemented their deeply felt alienation from the land through their cosmopolitan embrace of ecumenicism. The etymology of the word ecumenical—from the Greek *oikoumene*, 'inhabited land'—gives the best account of what this theology tries to correct. Imagining the unity of the world's faiths is an attempt on the part of the mystic to compensate for her voluntary divorce from habitation. She never leaves the earth, of course, she is still a finite person, but she does, in choosing God, permanently cease to inhabit the place where she was born. The secular, meanwhile, has never known any home but the land. She rejects the need for religious ecumenicism by appealing to an abstract concept of the human as the being gifted with thought. 'Empirical' discords within the category of the human alienate the secular from her self-abstraction, however. There are generic, racial, international conflicts; there are conflicting concepts of the human being itself, both ontological and political, that destabilize her felt connection to her home. She is as unconscious of her need for pluralism as the mystic is unconscious of her need for ecumenicism. Secularization is a reaction to the horror of empirical humanity—not only its violence, but also its unaccountable variety, which, if allowed to proliferate without regulation, threatens to contradict the accounting methods of reason. Thus pluralism, as the artificial outgrowth of secularism, does more than simply permit the coexistence of multiple absolute truths. It also announces the failure of universal abstractions to tally the inhabitants of secular land.

On mystical writing

1

It is not by mere preference that so much mystical writing is short-winded or fragmentary. Dealings with the absolute are necessarily indefinite. Indeed, it is because the infinite is indefinite that it can even be judged absolute, for inasmuch as it is not finite, it is also impossible to diminish. The absolute, then, is nothing total, but rather that which has gained integrity through the form of incompleteness. Tireless outpourings of words fail to grasp what is most graspable in the infinite, which is not its extension, but its lack of resolution. The fragment of thought is far more saturated with the infinite than the comprehensive tome, and this is because the form of the fragment is always purposive to its indefinite subject, while the tome is eager to exhaust the subject matter that it is helpless to dominate. The use of the fragment is more than a literary convenience for the mystic, therefore. It is as much as she can communicate in a single moment of suffering, an appropriately minimalist expression of her finitude.

2

If the mystic fails to establish a consistent vocabulary in her contemplations, this inconsistency does not reflect her lack of discipline so much as her permanent fixation upon the unutterable. Consider the history of that word 'fixation.' The word derives from the Latin *fixatio*, an alchemical term that, in one tradition, denotes the fifth of fourteenth stages for creating the *magnum opus*, or 'philosopher's stone.' The basic process of fixation is the reduction of a volatile spirit into a stable solid that cannot be unmade by fire. This is a crucial stage in the creation of the *magnum opus* because it brings a previously ethereal substance under control, 'fixing' it, so to speak, so that the material congelation of the stone can be realized in the ultimate stage. The uses of the word fixation have expanded in the modern science of psychology. The word has been appropriated in English translations of the writings of Sigmund Freud, in instances where the author tries to account for the anachronistic persistence into adulthood of infantile desires. Freud thought that 'fixation' was caused by one of two formative events: a lack of gratification in one of the early stages of psychosexual development, whereby the child fastens his unplacated feelings to a single object of desire; or, just the opposite, by a superabundance of psychosexual impressions which the child associates so strongly with a single object that he is unable to unlearn the association even upon reaching sexual maturity. Freudian fixation and alchemical fixation are alike in that they both involve bringing a previously volatile object under subjective control. In alchemy, this meant reducing a mercurial spirit into solid matter as a necessary stage in the materialization of the philosopher's stone. In psychoanalysis, it meant transforming an aggregation of confused childhood desires into an object that had a graspable reality for the subject. Mystical writing is an attempt at a synthesis of these two kinds of fixation.

On revelation

The original sources of revelation are ultimately apocryphal. In modern English, the word apocrypha functions in a double sense: first, as a derivative from the Latin word *apocrypha*, an ecclesiastical noun meaning 'hidden script.' Revelations are apocryphal inasmuch as their sources, which purport to be divine and ancient, cannot be adequately accounted for. There is no clear path to the beginning of revelations, and even if there was a strategy for tracking them, the way would be littered with glyphs and riddles. Now, the word apocrypha in its adjectival form has a second sense beyond the Latin, a sense of dubious authorship and truth-value—the 'apocryphal' anecdote, the fanciful tale. Reason rejects revelation on the basis of this twofold lack of credibility. It accuses the mystic of conflating the invisible with the accessible, the unaccountable with knowledge gained by hypothesis and experimentation. Its main objection is that the temporality of mystical thought does not 'check out' logically. Indeed, how can the mystical thinker claim to bring new knowledge into the world without first having put in the time-consuming, cognitive work? How can she claim to experience a pre-cognitive, apocryphal moment of judgment simultaneously with a counter-intuitive, reflective moment? By way of rebuttal, the mystic simply asks human reason to consider the apocryphal structure of reasoning itself. In Immanuel Kant's philosophy, for example, the achievement of rational self-consciousness depends upon a curious interaction between the transcendental infrastructure of reason and the self-activity of the thinker. Kant says in the *Critique of Pure Reason* that the mind intuits itself only as it is affected by itself; that the cognitive antecedent meets its consequences only after the latter has been quickened into motion by the senses. So the transcendental structure of cognition relates to reason in a way not very unlike the way divinity relates to revelation. But the mystic can appeal to a simpler example than this. What is an *education*, she asks, if not a divine procedure of generating reflective thought? Education is a process by which the counter-intuitive acquires the magical capability of appearing simultaneously with the pre-cognitive. This is not to say that education leaves no visible trail behind it; to be sure, the way of learning is littered with plenty of riddles and glyphs. But the mystery of the educative process is how it can leave a trail of textual clues that traces back to nowhere in particular. Name the precise moment that your education really begins–name that sublime origin of your thought, says the mystic to reason–and then you will have refuted my holy conceit.

Cherub

As your body steamed with fever,
your divine education endured with you as ice.
Long ago God prepared his ranking angels to
deliver you a sickle,
selecting the fiercest of his cherubs—
a bird with wings spread full distaff
and the radiation of the Holy Ghost teeming in
its mohawk.

It descended upon you out of the ceiling,
icicles like scythes depending from its wings,
yet unbending,
as if they were pendulums hinging the seconds
before the hour of God's killing judgment.
But you knew that His cherub would not bring
the gift of death:
For it comes to re-gift life to the death-willing.

three UN-EDUCATION

And who can think any advantages of fortune a sufficient compensation for the least breach of the social virtues, when he considers, that not only his character with regard to others, but also his peace and inward satisfaction entirely depend upon his strict observance of them; and that a mind will never be able to bear its own survey, that has been wanting in its part to mankind and society?

—David Hume, *A Treatise of Human Nature*

The School of Un-education

She who would be an educator in the twenty-first century graduates into a world of trillion-dollar debt and ruthless exploitation of global education markets by predatory capitalists. 'What good amid these?' she has every right to ask. And I would reply to her (who is just myself, reading with myself): 'None, but for a sentence of Virginia Woolf's.'

In the essay *A Room of One's Own*, first delivered in 1929 as the 'Women and Fiction' lectures at the Newnham and Girton Arts Societies in England, Virginia Woolf suggests, through the voice of a fictional lecturer, that the young women in the audience have come to university 'to become uneducated.' It seems an odd choice of words on first reading, yet considered in relation to the overall argument of the essay, the word un-education starts to sound very apropos. For it is the author's argument that the historical moment compels the women's college in England to formalize the process of un-learning–specifically, un-learning the fictions being propagated about women in the traditional men's colleges as well as the social institutions and mores of broader English society. The work of formal education for women must be, at least in part, to unmake minds, dissolving the nefarious aspects of publicly inherited knowledges in order to re-form those knowledges in view of those buried truths that for centuries safeguarded the ideal of social justice from the unrelenting cognitive violence of sexism.

We can read the women's college in *A Room of One's Own* not only as a rising institution of Interwar England, then, but as a fictional figuration, the literary reaching beyond its historical closure into imaginable futures. My hunch is that Woolf's figuration of the women's college is less concerned with abstract idealities than with the real possibilities of the historical moment. Her notion of 'un-education' imagines the school's redemption in a political context where it has primarily functioned as a conservative counterweight to justice. She envisions a higher education curriculum whose positive program is the negation of the cognitive damages caused by centuries of epistemic violence. But she demands even more than this. She asks for the school of un-learning to be rigorously formalized, to become a permanent, counterintuitive force in public life, to heal the deepest-seated of all civil wounds–the divorce of the literary imagination from proper knowledge.

It would be a mistake to read the narrator's proposal as some kind of naive educational idealism. Neither should it be taken for a stoical optimism. Woolf never understates the costs (and I do not mean monetary) of becoming 'un-educated.' For starters, the un-educated person must forsake her home in the familiar world of her childhood in favor of a world of credentials and cold competition. Her intellectual empowerment at school is at the same time an entrance into a certain kind of 'ignorance,' for at present there are no set curricula for her future studies, nor guarantors for her worldly success. There is a double onus on her to prove to the so-called 'educated' crowd that her institutional pedigree is as legitimate as theirs. So this is not educational idealism. Nor is there any tragic optimism here. If anything, Woolf is making a call for self-endangerment for the sake of a notion of justice that assumes as one of its necessary conditions the transformation of certain kinds of 'ignorance' into formidable bodies of knowledge.

Insofar as we can still point to those elements within the school (or the university) that engender the intellectual conditions Woolf describes in *A Room of One's Own*, then there is still a possibility–let us not conflate it with a hope–that her visionary, un-educational revolution could take place

Who is the public intellectual of democracy?

As far back as 1835, Alexis de Tocqueville, writing of America, observed that the social positioning of its professional intellectuals put them in a strained relationship with that amorphous and powerful entity he famously called 'the majority.' He discerned as only a liberal European aristocrat could that liberated individual reason had come to substitute for an ecclesiastical intelligentsia in the rising mass citizenry of Jacksonian Democracy. Radical equality in politics now entailed radical equality in judgment. The amount of influence that one citizen's judgments had on another's was, according to the French political scientist, 'of necessity much curtailed in a country where [people returned constantly] to their own rationality as to the most obvious and immediate source of truth.' In a nation where no citizen was viewed as superior in knowledge or rank to any other, no predilection existed to take the word of one person over another's. This radically egalitarian, anti-intellectualist ethos created two conflicting tendencies in the free population of America. One, Tocqueville observed, which

> leads every man's thought into new paths[,] aand another which force[s] him willingly to cease thinking at all. Beneath the power of certain laws, democracy... blot[s] out that intellectual liberty supported by the [...] state in such a way that, having broken the shackles formerly imposed upon it by class systems or [other] men, the human spirit [becomes] closely confined by the general will of the majority.

I wonder what can be learned about the personality of the public intellectual in the United States by taking up Tocqueville's formulation of democracy's cognitive dilemma. Democrats, he insisted, are mistrustful, and democrats are unthinking. And this was not simply a matter of rude individualism offending an aristocrat's sensibilities. Tocqueville was not lamenting the selfish willfulness of the citizen so much as the cognitive damage he incurred from his equality with his peers. The nascent Jacksonian Democracy was teaching the individual how to hate the despotic person, but it was not teaching her how to hate the despotic thought. Here, then, was an opportunity for a figure like the concerned public intellectual to become influential in the life of the people. By defining the intellectual dilemma of equality, Tocqueville had outlined for her a twofold task: on the one hand, to endorse the radical equality that had liberated individual judgment from the feudal king's; on the other hand, to rebel against the compulsory conformism that re-enslaved judgment under the very conditions of its emancipation. Equal parts participant and critic, therefore, Tocqueville's public intellectual would have dwelled in that unexplored space between alignment and alienation, pledging her allegiance to a public that did not resemble a national body politic so much as an ideal cognitive commons -- a public of the imagination where she could have expressed her concern for equality, as well as her longing for freedom, without contradiction.

Discussion note from a reading group of left-wing educators

In the *Prison Notebooks*, Antonio Gramsci theorizes an 'intermediate element' between the party leadership and the massive base that 'maintains contact between them, not only physically but also morally and intellectually.' No doubt he is referring to the educative activity of the party's intellectuals, without which the party cannot make a legitimate claim to represent the masses. This intermediate, *educative* element is what reorganizes and matures the party when a particular phase of its leadership falters and wanes. With a better-educated base, Gramsci's theory goes, the next phase of party life can be built on the *ruins* of the previous one.

Gramsci further elaborates this point when he says that the party leadership should be assessed according to two criteria, '1. in what it actually does; 2. in what provision it makes for the eventuality of its own destruction.' The educative activity of the party, therefore, is equal parts positive and negative. All the while that it is creating a heritage among the masses through education, it is simultaneously attending to its own dissolution. Thus, in its educative contact with the lower-classes, the party should be doing violence to its own organized element. Gramsci's paradoxical point is that the party's organization can only be achieved once it has un-organized itself and allowed for the emergent generation to reconstruct it. *Liberal institutional idealism* is categorically left out of this conception of the political party.

Recovered computer file: 'Unexpected affinities of a poet and a logician'

By a fortunate accident I recently read, in quick succession, two books that started a conversation in my thoughts about the manner in which education calls individuals into commerce with universal objects. The two texts were Friedrich Schiller's *Letters on the Aesthetic Education of Man* (1795) and John Stuart Mill's *Autobiography* (1873). Schiller's text shows the effort of a disenchanted poet to compose a philosophical treatise on the potential of the aesthetic sense to steward the political education of humanity. Mill's text, on the other hand, offers the romantic reflections of a logician who, facing the dusk of an accomplished life in thought, is finally sitting down to record for posterity's sake the history of his unconventional education.

Prima facie, the two books—the two authors as men—seem to have nothing substantive in common. It must have been the fortunate timing of my reading that enabled me to generate the following question that unifies them: how does the education of individuals bring them into awareness (or non-awareness) of universal political objects?

Now, I might have expected Schiller, the rebellious German poet with no formal philosophical training, to take up my question 'poetically'; and Mill, the English bureaucrat with a lifetime of schooling in formal logic and classical Greek, to take it up 'logically.' Yet it was

Schiller who, in important respects, turned out to be the more logical, while Mill, in his turn, proved to be the greater poet. Both argued that it would be a mistake for humanistic education to reinforce the division of the mind into counterpoised 'rational' and 'sensuous' elements. The twain must invariably meet (if not in education, then in the inevitable mental crisis that follows the completion of it), and it is only through such a meeting that political subjects in large modern societies learn to grasp the abstract universal as their own.

How do Schiller's *Letters* make the case that education, specifically 'aesthetic' education, brings individuals into conscious participation in universal activities?

> Though need may drive Man into society, and Reason implant social principles in him, Beauty alone can confer upon him a social character. Taste alone brings harmony into society, because it establishes harmony in the individual. All other forms of perception divide a man, because they are exclusively based either on the sensuous or on the intellectual part of his being; only the perception of the beautiful makes something whole of him, because both his natures must accord with it.

Here we have a systematic account of how an aesthetic education raises individuals into their truly social (for Schiller, this means truly *free*) character. The three spheres of the mind—described above as sensuousness, Beauty, and intellect—all exist *a priori*, though in order for an individual's imagination to flourish, he must properly activate the third sphere, the Beautiful sphere. He does this by disciplining his capricious nature and relaxing his computational brain. This idealized reconciliation of his personality makes him a better-rounded, more complete political self, fully developed in his own nature and in relationship to his peers.

Schiller counterpoises his concept of aesthetic education to the economical concept of utility which, in his view, has become the 'great idol' of the eighteenth century. Yet here is where J.S. Mill, the lifelong utilitarian, makes an unexpected contribution to Schiller's discussion. In the *Autobiography*, Mill confesses the tendency of the utilitarian philosophy to be unfeeling and hyper-rational in its explication of human motives, suggesting, even, that it may be misguided in its methodical delineation of the causes of pleasure and pain in human actions. In short, for Mill, utilitarianism neglects an 'education of the feelings' and needs to be supplemented by a curriculum that meets that undeniable human need.

Mill's conviction follows from a mental crisis that he suffered when he was twenty years old. It was then that he started to consider that the accelerated development of his mental powers at such a tender age (John's father, James, started him on a strict regimen of classical Greek when he was still a babbling toddler) might have been inhibiting his capacity as an adult to invest authentic emotion in his objects of study. Once the time had come to evaluate what his political commitments truly meant to him, Mill found himself checking his motives at the door. Was his individual satisfaction and happiness (the chief ends of all human conduct, according to the utilitarian philosophy) at all connected to his pursuit of technical solutions to social problems? He felt compelled to answer in the negative, arriving at the following life-redirecting insight:

> I never, indeed, wavered in the conviction that happiness is the test of all rules of conduct, and the end of life. But I now thought that this end was only to be attained by not making it the direct end. Those only are happy (I thought) who have their minds fixed on some object other than their own happiness; on the happiness of others, on the improvement of mankind, even on some art or pursuit, followed not as a means, but as itself an ideal end. Aiming thus at something else, they find happiness by the way.

Thus did an accomplished student of political economy and formal logic find a way out of mental crisis—by identifying in his emotional turmoil a jagged pathway to universal objects. But he was only able to make this identification after he recognized that he had been over-nurtured in analysis and under-nurtured in his poetical sense:

> I had now learnt by experience that the passive susceptibilities needed to be cultivated as well as the active capacities, and required to be nourished and enriched as well as guided. I did not, for an instant, lose sight of, or undervalue, that part of the truth which I had seen before; I never turned recreant to intellectual culture, or ceased to consider the power and practice of analysis as an essential condition both of individual and of social improvement. But I thought that it had consequences which required to be corrected, by joining other kinds of cultivation with it. The maintenance of a due balance among the faculties, now seemed to me of primary importance. The cultivation of the feelings [through poetry] became one of the cardinal points in my ethical and philosophical creed.

Mill finds common ground with Schiller regarding the necessity of educating the aesthetic sensibility, albeit on the basis of a cooked-down utilitarian principle that individual lives cannot attain maximum fulfillment without achieving a proper equilibrium of analysis and feeling. Still, Mill's recognition that there was an artificial division between logic and emotion in his education clarifies a shortcoming in the utilitarian philosophy of education more generally; and through the apprehension of the *aesthetic*, he learns how to identify his personal satisfaction with his aims as a social thinker. This is not entirely unlike Schiller's program, which works the same concern from a different angle, and with respect to a different crisis (the 1789 revolution in France).

In summary, then, both thinkers arrive at a defense of aesthetic education through the 'wrong' (the under-nurtured) sides of their intellects—Schiller through philosophy, Mill through poetry. Crucial to note here is the point made by both writers that the value of an individual's education can only be measured in terms of the universal objects with which he identifies, and that the fate of the universal plays out not only on the grand political stage, but likewise in the *cognitive development of every individual*.

Some ideas for a critique of killing animals

1

TWO MOMENTS OF VIOLENCE. A true critique of the subject of killing animals would have to examine its relation to the political structuring of human violence. Where similar critiques have erred is in their failure to recognize that the enforced distinction between the 'sacredly' human and the 'profanely' animal is neither metaphysical nor biological, but legal, sovereign. The continuation of natural violence against nonhumans into a legal order that prohibits natural violence between human beings ought to be conceived of as a moment of *humanizing* violence. The legal ban on natural violence in the human sphere is put in place to distract from its normalization in the Darwinian sphere. We overcome the pre-political 'state of nature' amongst ourselves by upholding it in relation to every other living thing. This *humanizing* moment of violence contrasts with a simultaneous, *dehumanizing* moment that is characteristic of all political domination, specifically, the state's inevitable interference in the popular mental struggle to imagine a more perfect justice than the one currently being enforced as if by fate. What eventually comes to be mystified as inviolable, 'sacred' humanity is actually just an ad hoc fusion of these *humanizing* and *dehumanizing* moments of violence.

2

COLONIALISM. Consider a scene of animal killing from a famous political parable by George Orwell called 'Shooting an Elephant.' The narrator of the parable is a colonial police officer serving in a rural village in British-controlled Lower Burma who has become disenchanted with the colonial bureaucracy as well as the perverse politics of Western dominion in the East. The officer thinks imperialism an evil enterprise; he believes he sympathizes with the Burman oppressed. He feels silenced, moreover, by his duty to serve the empire. 'But I could get nothing into perspective,' he writes at the beginning of his story, 'I was young and ill-educated and I had had to think out my problems in the utter silence that is imposed on every Englishman in the East.'

The plot of 'Shooting an Elephant' follows the escape of a laboring elephant from its master's home. One morning, the elephant breaks loose from its chains and starts running amok in the busiest parts of the village. It wreaks havoc in the main residential and commercial districts, at one point squashing a Dravidian coolie man under its huge foot, then flees into the rice fields beyond the village. As the on-duty officer that day, the narrator is charged with subduing the elephant and bringing chaos back to order. Initially, he hopes that he will be able to corral the distressed animal and return it to its owner with minimal damage to human life and property. The situation starts to spiral out of his control, however, when a crowd of Burman villagers—two thousand strong, according to the text—amasses behind the narrator hoping to see him dispense of the elephant in brutal fashion. The narrator admits that he does not want to shoot the beast—knows he ought not shoot it, given the value of its labor—but he feels the univocal will of the crowd urging him on, irresistibly. '[I]t was at this moment,' he writes, 'as I stood there with the rifle in my hands, that I first grasped the hollowness of the white man's dominion in the East. Here was I, the white man with his gun, standing in front of the unarmed native crowd—seemingly the leading actor of the piece; but in reality I was only an absurd puppet pushed to and fro by the will of those yellow faces behind. I perceived in this moment that when the white man turns tyrant it is his own freedom that he destroys...He wears a mask, and his face grows to fit it.'

The narrator shoots the elephant in the head once, twice, three times, but the beast's massive body does not concede the battle right away. Instead, an 'enormous senility [settles] upon [the elephant],' whereupon it falls to the ground and begins the slow, agonizing process of dying. It takes a full thirty minutes for the narrator's bullets to achieve their purpose, a duration for which he does not have the stomach to stand by and wait. He returns to his post rather shaken by the ordeal, consoled only by his recollection of the dead coolie man, an incident that gives him a legitimate pretext to his superiors for having shot down such a valuable piece of property.

Orwell discloses two important political relationships in his morbid parable. The first is the relationship of the narrator to the crowd of 'yellow faces' that coerces him into shooting the elephant. That the Burman villagers manage to achieve critical mass in their exploited position is a significant detail of the story, since, presumably, the colonial police force is there to keep the people as collectively ineffectual as possible. Once amassed, the crowd asserts a powerful, though distorted, sovereignty over the narrator who, caught in the 'bloodthirsty' gaze of their 'yellow faces,' suddenly realizes the futility of British rule in the East. He sees that he can have no freedom in his mindless, weaponized role as a colonial policeman. There is no choice left him but to placate the people's desire to see the elephant slaughtered. He gives them the spectacle they demand, though it is amply clear, by the end, that the slain elephant is merely a convenient substitute for the other dying beast in the background—British imperial rule.

The distorted, provisional sovereignty of the colonized Burmans frames a second, subtler relation between the narrator and the elephant. The two beings share the experience of being silenced by others. The narrator, as

I mentioned, is silenced from two opposing directions: by his superior officers whose orders transform him from a thinking man to an armed automaton; and by the Burman villagers, whose long-thwarted will to violence (against their oppressors, against nature itself) overrides his wish to subdue the elephant without murdering it. His only means of communicating with the elephant, therefore, is inhuman, through the pre-linguistic idiom of natural violence. The elephant responds to the narrator's violence with its own form of silenced 'speech'—the breathless, tortured gasps that so disturb the narrator's conscience that he has to abandon the scene before the creature is dead.

A conventional man-versus-nature reading is impossible in the case of Orwell's 'Shooting an Elephant.' Here we witness a transaction between a human being and an animal that could only have taken place in the jurisdiction of an illegitimate colonial sovereign.

3

POSTCOLONIALISM. J.M. Coetzee's *Disgrace* is a novel about unpardonable secular sins. Set in post-Apartheid South Africa, the plot follows a middle-aged, white South African man named David Lurie, an unemployed ex-professor who experiences total personal upheaval at a moment when the nation's institutions are trying to work out a historic, de-racialized redistribution of political power.

There are as many layers to David Lurie's disgrace as there are episodes in the novel. The main drama begins when David initiates a liaison with one of his pupils at the technical university where he teaches, a young woman who ends up emotionally damaged by their interactions. The university forces David, rather publicly, out of his teaching post, after which he travels to the Eastern Cape for an extended stay with his daughter, Lucy. Not long after David arrives at Lucy's, her farm, which doubles as a dog kennel, gets raided by three black men who pillage the house and murder all of the kenneled dogs in brutal fashion. The men conclude the raid by setting fire to David's clothes and gang-raping Lucy. In the aftermath of these horrors, David and Lucy struggle to rebuild their relationship on liveable terms. Lucy ends up pregnant by the rape, and decides, against her father's counsel, to have the child, entering into a marriage of convenience with her black neighbor, Petrus, who offers her physical protection in exchange for the deed of her land. Although David protests his daughter's choices, he also knows that he is too physically and spiritually scarred by his experiences to be of help to her himself. The fiasco at the university and the racially charged catastrophe at the farm have left him virtually ineffectual, and he must find a way to put his own life back together before he can once more play a part in his daughter's.

While all of is going on in the foreground of the plot, in the background civil relations in the Eastern Cape are growing more precarious by the day. The bitter lesson of Coetzee's novel seems to be that disgrace compounds disgrace. There is no way out of trouble for David; at every desperate turn of the plot, he confronts the cold truth of his personal and social sins, knowing full well that there is no absolution waiting for him at the end of his struggle—only more truths, more miseries. This is where the trope of killing animals comes to the fore of *Disgrace*. After the brutal raid on Lucy's home, David takes up volunteering at a local animal shelter, where he assists a woman named Bev with pet euthanasias. These tender scenes of mercy killing at the shelter offset the cold-blooded butchery of the earlier raid scene. For whereas the raid exemplified the easy degeneration of political chaos into natural violence (the substitution of one form of brutality for another), the euthanasia scenes suggest the possibility of restoring some semblance of humanity to a white-supremacist South African society. David Lurie learns in the course of his volunteer work that putting dying animals to death under the correct auspices is a means for him to transmogrify the ugly remnants of Apartheid violence into a more humane form of care.

'Love' is the name that David gives to animal euthanasia at the end of the novel. Still, there is a deep sense of infelicity in this secular rite of sacrifice, a nagging feeling that the sacrificer will never appease the 'higher power' (God? the new South Africa?) that solicits a sacrifice from him. We see this most poignantly in the final scene of the novel, where David prepares a tumor-ridden little dog with which he has made a special bond:

> He (David) opens the cage door. 'Come,' he says, bends, opens his arms. The dog wags its crippled rear, sniffs his face, licks his cheeks, his lips, his ears. He does nothing to stop it. 'Come.'
>
> Bearing him in his arms like a lamb, he re-enters the surgery. 'I thought you would save him for another week,' says Bev Shaw. 'Are you giving him up?'
>
> 'Yes, I am giving him up.'

The soberness of Coetzee's art is most affecting in scenes like this one, where the moment would be lost entirely to sentimentality if not for the subversive grammar of the final quotation—'I am giving him up,' uttered in the perfective tense, signalling a completed action. Coetzee's subtle suggestion here is that David completes the act of sacrifice without *himself* being completed by it. He continues on in a state of disgrace, of original sin without pardon, the spiritual condition of a guilty white man in an emergent postcolonial order. Even the lamblike little dog that serves as David's sacrificial object does not complete the perfective tense of the scene. It is not like the lambs once taken to the Holy Temple in Jerusalem for ritual sacrifice according to the ancient Mosaic Laws, nor is it intended to be a humble symbol of Christ dying on the cross for the sins of the world. The killing of the animal, though supervised under humane conditions, has no significance beyond the room in which it happens. The irreplaceable life extinguished in the surgery does not—cannot—substitute for the life of the sinner that gives it up. At best, it offers him a lesson in how he might dignify his disgrace in the face of a world that cannot forgive his condition.

4

CAPITALIST-DEMOCRACY. A rainy evening in October, 2011. A troubled man of middle age reveals to an astonished world that he has been hording a veritable Noah's Ark of creatures on his private acreage at 270 Kopchak Road, Zanesville, Ohio, USA. In the last bitter act before his suicide, Terry Thompson opens the cage doors of fifty African lions, Bengal tigers, grizzly bears, great apes, and wolves, releasing a malnourished horde of carnivores into an unsuspecting upper Appalachian community of farmers and light-manufacturing workers.

What follows from Thompson's madness is one of the most legendary fugitive hunts in American history. As the sky blackens over Zanesville, the local sheriff's office (better trained to deal with traffic collisions and domestic disputes than zoological crises), dispatches its entire on- and off-duty forces into the hills surrounding Thompson's property, with the desperate goal of getting control of the crisis by the next morning. By some miracle they succeed, finding and killing every animal that Thompson set loose the previous evening, save the lone baboon, which they believe to have met its demise between the gaping jaws of an African lion.

Come morning, the police are loath to speak of the horrors they had to commit in the woods overnight. Stories that just twenty-four hours before would have sounded like whoppers from a hunting vacation gone awry—tall tales of one-on-one melees with charging grizzlies and rabid wolves—have suddenly become, after the turning of Terry Thompson's key, not only conceivable, but believable. Yet somehow, these unspeakable experiences have to be presented as palatable to the global mass media, which, once it catches wind of the story, is sure to swarm Zanesville like a plague of locusts. The deputy sheriff overseeing the massacre recognizes the need for a more seasoned spokesperson than himself to fend off the inquiring media, an expert who will understand the magnitude of the situation and stand beside the actions of local law enforcement. In a stroke of pure political genius, he summons the charismatic, straight-talking 'Jungle' Jack Hanna, the *Late Show* animal guru who has close ties to the State of Ohio through his directorship of the world-renowned Columbus Zoo.

Within hours of being summoned away from a speaking tour in the Northeast, Hanna gains control of the master media narrative and never relinquishes it. His main challenge is to combat the vitriolic reactions on the Internet to an iconic photograph taken at the scene at

270 Kopchak Road, showing dozens of beautiful, bullet-riddled tiger carcasses soaking in rust-colored puddles of blood and mud and rain, a lone human figure standing tall amid the carnage. Hanna uses the same fast-talking, plain-folks manners on which he has staked his television persona. *This was like Noah's Ark being released in the middle of Ohio,* he tells one CNN, MSNBC, CBS News reporter after another. *What would you have said to the parents of the child who got maimed by a lioness at the bus stop?* And so on, in a series of controversy-killing non-sequiturs that not only convinces the media to step off, but apparently discourages them from doing any serious philosophizing about the massacre. *A bad man and some bad laws are to blame for the Zanesville tragedy. But now the bad man is dead, and the laws are going to change, so let's agree to bury this case with the animals and make sure it never happens again.*

Of course the enduring horror of the Zanesville Zoo Massacre has less to do with Hanna's oversimplifying narrative (after all, what feeling person would choose the life of a lioness over that of a defenseless child?), and more to do with the media's intellectual incapacity to probe deeper into the philosophical questions raised by the event. Was Jack Hanna's perspective on exotic animal stewardship *so* unlike Terry Thompson's that the media could afford to ignore the similarities? Did not both men fashion themselves as representatives (obviously with drastically different codes of ethics) of the view that a 'domesticated' animal kingdom could dwell benignly within advanced capitalist democracy? Would not both men have agreed that the private breeding of exotic animals, whether in zoos or in the homes of 'responsible' owners, presented a unique opportunity to merge the laws of the innermost jungle with Western man's inalienable right to cultivate property?

The irony for the Zanesville animals was that, when catastrophe struck, the open wilds of American democracy proved far deadlier than the jungles of 'darkest Africa' from whence their unlucky ancestors were plucked. Terry Thompson may well have been on a maniacal mission, but his insanity, in retrospect, seems more intelligible than our outrage. At least Thompson understood the undisguised barbaric character of his occupation. His last living action was, at bottom, an attempt at a full self-disclosure, a candid taunt to the world of good conscience of which he seemed to discount himself a member. *Look*, he seemed to say to his demoralized audience, *look at the sheer terror I have at my command*.

Democracy, Tragedy, Metonymy

I. The Two Poles of Tragedy

We are speaking today on literature and social justice. Perhaps this task would be less difficult for me were I sure that literature should serve social justice, or that a just world would produce fine literature, but I am not so sure of either. Of literature that purports to serve social justice causes, I seem to reserve a special skepticism, and I will not speak about the literature of a just world, since I have no experience of such a place. On occasions like this, my thoughts turn to Friedrich von Schiller, the German poet who wrote in the wake of the French Revolution that the greatest work of art we can imagine would be the building up of a true political freedom for all humanity. One has to examine that claim carefully. Schiller was not saying that great art will help us govern, or, as I thought when I first read him, that politics will make us better artists. He was suggesting, rather, that an emancipated humanity would study freedom as an art, and, in time, make freedom its finest art. Believing this at the historical moment that he did must have put Schiller in a very disconsolate mood. Still, if all life is an animal farm, then I think of Schiller as having been most like the goat, singing with his fellow animals when they were joyful, and bleating with them when they had their throats cut. He wrote tragedies on the incompatibility of the noble passions with the frozen institutions of feudalism, though unlike, say, the tragedies of Shakespeare, Schiller's tragedies were more likely to culminate with the hero submitting himself, as in *The Robbers*, to be judged under the formal legal process, rather than under the jealous sword, for his main preoccupation, in lieu of metaphysical man, was political man, i.e., man who could conceive of liberty and equality concomitantly with the guillotine.

Bloody and inconclusive was the democratic revolution in Europe at the time of Schiller's death in 1805. His learned analogy, late in life, of democracy to the form of tragedy, was as historically as it was philosophically motivated. As Schiller saw it, man had successfully reasoned out the idea of equality in philosophy, yet in practice had proven tragically underprepared to realize it (hope for America was a generation away for many European democrats). It is interesting to compare the tragic liberalism of an early modern like Friedrich von Schiller, a German, to that of a later modern like Sir Isaiah Berlin, a Russo-English Jew who lived long enough to view the bloody upheavals of the Twentieth Century in hindsight. Berlin was not, as far as I know, an avid commentator on Schiller, but he did look to the flowering of Weimar Classicism for constant inspiration. In particular, Berlin was fond of J.G. von Herder's nascent value pluralism (often misidentified as cultural relativism), as well as one of Immanuel Kant's more poetic turns of phrase, in which the philosopher observed that out of the crooked timber of humanity, no straight thing was ever made. Indeed, Herder's doctrine of 'incommensurable objectivities' and Kant's one-liner contained the same positive observation; that man, at any given time, pursues so many uncommon ends that he cannot possibly make them all agree. Held up to the light of the Twentieth Century, which in Berlin's review reads like one sustained attempt to 'straighten the timber,' Herder and Kant's claims begin to ring with tragic sentiment. Berlin's late modernist revision of an older value pluralism was nothing if not a tragic philosophy developed out of witnessing humanity fall, not only from the high seat of Reason, but from the End of History itself. Every liberal in the West agreed that bringing Utopia down to Earth had brought catastrophic results. Only by returning to the Middle of History, where absolute values were volatile, refutable, and above all impermanent, was there any hope of making a fresh start in the postwar world order.

With the lessons of the first half of the Twentieth Century, Berlin improved Schiller's uncompleted tragic play into a cogent philosophical treatise. During the early modern round of revolution, Schiller understood democratic tragedy solely in terms of man's unworthiness before his new political ideal. Berlin, by the third or fourth round of blood and inconclusion, saw democratic tragedy as the permanent condition of free men, a struggle not of ultimate ideals, but of incommensurable values. Which absolutes are appealing, which appalling? That we even have to ask the question, again and again, is a tragedy in itself, for it suggests, first, that man is not improving morally with each passing generation, yet lives, at all times, in danger of regressing; second, it suggests that man does not have an earthly destiny, an End of History, waiting for him at the end of his struggle. Even so, for Berlin, it was better to have to sort through the good and the bad, mindful of vulgar, empirical humanity, than to take lives in the name of an absolute. 'To demand more than [the opportunity to stand unflinchingly for the relative validity of one's convictions] is perhaps a deep and incurable metaphysical need,' he writes at the end of 'Two Concepts of Liberty'; 'but to allow it to determine one's practice is a symptom of an equally deep, and more dangerous, moral and political immaturity.'

Let me return to the question of freedom with which I opened. How did an early modern tragedian like Schiller view the experience of freedom compared to a late modern liberal like Berlin? The difference between them can be explained with Berlin's own formula of 'positive' versus 'negative' liberty. Whereas Schiller fits with his contemporary, Kant, into the tradition of 'positive' liberty as self-mastery, a tradition that, Berlin notes ironically, puts less emphasis on the the possibilities than on the limits of human self-knowledge (all that we cannot, and should not, try to master); Berlin, by contrast, was heir to the English liberalism of John Stuart Mill, a school that emphasized the negative, so-called 'freedom from,' pole of liberty. Now, my grouping of Schiller and Berlin into 'positive' and 'negative' poles is less for precision's sake than for the purpose of trying to discern what lies between them. For there seems to have been a shift, from the earlier to the later modern, in the orientation of the individual toward the institutions, as well as the citizens, of mass society. Schiller assumed that the experience of freedom obtained exclusively in the mutual cancellation of the 'sensuous' and 'rational' halves of the personality. 'Positive' freedom was the individual's experience of setting himself free from the divergent dictates of nature and reason. Schiller's revised Kantianism held that the individual should design his personality in accordance with this idealized reconciliation of his divided subjectivity, disciplining his capricious nature, and relaxing his computational brain, on the way to becoming a more complete political self. Berlin had a historically altered set of concerns. His 'negative' defense of liberty emerged from the shadows of European, and to an extent, East Asian, totalitarianism. His chief concern was that self-possessed individuals not be killed, one by one or en masse, by absolute authorities. For him, the peaceful coexistence of incommensurable values was preferable to the promotion of a single absolute. Individual freedom became about balancing self-mastery with social awareness. If I am to coexist even with my most estranged neighbors, it is my responsibility at least to tolerate them. I must therefore make some effort to 'enter into' their world of values and judge the good and bad in them as best I can. More important than agreeing with my neighbor's values is recognizing them as legitimate *human* values that, insofar as they do not endanger the liberty of others, even though I may find them repugnant, are no less valid for repelling me. Note how the earlier modern, Schiller, was obsessed with perfecting human nature, while the later modern, Berlin, was obsessed with merely acknowledging it.

My question today is whether there were alternative forms of 'tragic' democratic liberalism between these positive and negative poles represented by Schiller and Berlin. Were there, in the modern Western history of ideas, articulations of individual freedom that fell somewhere between rational self-mastery and negative tolerance, borrowing elements of each, while creating something distinct from them? There was such a tradition, I will argue, in the United States. Let me be clear in saying that I am not advocating for any kind of American exceptionalism here, not in the least. If I intend anything, it is to provincialize Schiller and Berlin's views on liberty within their European contexts, and to do the same with the American writers

I am about to discuss. My aim is not to show that these figures have nothing in common, but that, even while they played provincial roles in the world-historical drama, they shared all too much in the way of tragedy.

II. *The American Art of Metonymy*

Before I go on, I ask you to reflect on a Tragic American Century that unfolded between the early and late phases of modern Europe, a century wedged between Friedrich von Schiller and Isaiah Berlin which the former could not have anticipated, and the latter could absorb but impressionistically into his project. It would be unfair to say that they or similarly positioned European critics 'missed' this phenomenon as they were fixed in contemplation of their home continent, but it is perfectly fair to say that the domestic battles of American democracy were a peripheral concern for them. The same provincialism of which I accuse European critics I also accuse the Americans I am about to discuss. But I think it worth commenting that, between the early modern period in Europe that anticipated fascist and communist totalitarianisms, and the late modern period that actualized them, a span of time over which European critical theorists have obsessed for more than half a century, there was an entire century in the United States dedicated to the egalitarian inclusion, as well as the ruthless suppression, of racial minorities—notably the descendents of African American slaves, but others as well—within mainstream democracy. This pivotal century spanned from the 1860s, the decade of the Civil War and Emancipation, to the 1960s, the decade of Civil Rights and the Culture Wars. It was tragic in both of the senses I have already discussed: in Schiller's sense of proving inadequate to its own democratic ideal, in the institutions of Jim Crow, labor oppression, anti-Communism, and other ills; and in Berlin's sense of having to learn tolerance from the deadly consequences of intolerance, as seen from the culture of lynching to the segregation of the public schools. But it was also much more than these, and I am not going to pretend to summarize a hundred years in an essay as brief as this one. So let me step out of the historians' circle, in which I feel very uncomfortable, and enter the circle of literature, where I would like to speak about two artists who wrote eloquently from either pole of the Tragic American Century.

The two artists I am referring to are Walt Whitman and Ralph Ellison, writers who lived under historical circumstances so parallel that their lives, in retrospect, seem cosmically bound together. Ninety-five years separated their births; one hundred two years their deaths; ninety-seven years the publication of their seminal works; and ninety-nine years the most important political revolutions of their times. Both were stewards of the democratic ideal during a century that was largely antagonistic to it. Whitman was a pre-

Emancipation writer who bloomed during the Civil War and waned during the Reconstruction. Ellison was a pre-Civil Rights writer who bloomed during the Sixties and waned during the Reagan Counterrevolution. Their writings merged in a single theme: the reconciliation of transcendental individuality with mass democracy. Whereas Whitman framed this reconciliation as the work of 'recorders ages hence,' Ralph Ellison turned to Whitman's generation for a precedent to uplift him.

A look at a few of their signature symbols will illustrate how I am framing these authors. Consider Whitman's poem, 'The Dalliance of the Eagles,' in which two eagles, representing two autonomous individualities, collide in mid-air as 'Four beating wings, two beaks, a swirling mass tight grappling.../the twain yet one, a moment's lull.../...then parting.../[in] separate diverse flight,/She hers, he his, pursuing.' The sudden amorous contact of the eagles suggests a transitory meeting of two personalities on divergent yet complementary trajectories. Now compare to Ellison's recurring figure of the jazz player, the utterly autonomous instrumentalist who seeks his freedom in the fugitive harmonies of combination play, one moment conforming to the group objective, the next retreating into a chaos of improvisational narcissism. The jazz player moves on the same trajectory as the eagle, the individual colliding with the swirling mass, 'the twain yet one,' harmonizing, then parting; as if the important thing was not the idiosyncrasy of the individual, but her very substitutability; as if social roles were merely to be taken up at serendipitous moments, then abandoned in pursuit of other freedoms.

I have taken to calling this shared trope of Whitman and Ellison's *metonymy*, or the art of substituting names. The eagle and the jazz player are metonyms, names that invoke the reconciliation between transcendental individuality and democracy. Both Whitman and Ellison are conscious of the impermanence of such names. Whitman's eagles grapple for a mere 'moment's lull' before breaking apart; Ellison's jazz player wheels forward for a spotlight solo only to hurry back in the darkness. By metonymy, then, I mean the symbolic naming of a form of freedom that cannot be experienced permanently.

Whitman writes, in the opening couplet of *Leaves of Grass*, 'One's self I sing, a simple separate person,/ Yet utter the word Democratic, the word En-Masse,' as if he already knew of that ultimate reconciliation for which, later in the book, he will substitute a thousand different names—self, En-Masse, the leaves of grass, the eagles, the black slave, the map of America, and, not least, his own name. But what about these names? Does this inexhaustible chain of metonyms not suggest a fundamental discontinuity between the poet and his ideal? If there is one danger in Whitman's art of substitution, it is that no name holds valid over any other. For what signifies in his metonym is less the name itself than the purposiveness of its form. The purposive usage of the name invokes the democratic ideal without fully disclosing it. The paradox of Whitman's effusive naming is that he actually imposes incredible constraints upon himself. His verbal inexhaustibility is a function of his inability to disclose the final form of the reconciliation he imagines. The more I read him, the more I believe that his readers should be substituting questions wherever we find declarations on the page. Rephrased as a question, the opening couplet of *Leaves of Grass* might read, 'How to sing my separate self while also speaking for you, the En-Masse?'

This is the question that in Whitman's prose writings gets worked out into the concept of 'democratic personalism.' It is the poet's most precise term for individual liberty:

> To [personalism], all bends; and it is because toward such result democracy alone, on anything like Nature's scale, breaks up the limitless fallows of humankind, and plants the seed, and gives fair play, that its claims now precede the rest. The literature, songs, esthetics, &c., of a country are of importance principally because they furnish the materials and suggestions of personality for the women and men of that country, and enforce them in a thousand effective ways…Bibles may convey, and priests expound, but it is exclusively for the noiseless operation of one's isolated Self, to enter the pure ether of veneration, reach the divine levels, and commune with the unutterable.

To which Whitman attaches the footnote: 'After the rest is satiated, all interest culminates in the field of persons, and never flags there.' In other words, democracy serves the interest of personalism, 'bends' to it as its inevitable best result. It is the political system that, by giving 'fair (and equal) play' to all personalities, is singularly capable of actuating their full potential. Yet it is through the personality alone, 'one's isolated Self,' says Whitman, that it is even possible to 'commune with the unutterable.' Here we run into a paradox. If political equality is the precondition for the flourishing of personalities, then the concept of personalism must have a healthy reciprocity with the concept of democracy. Democracy is necessarily the 'unutterable' poetic ideal to which Whitman refers, for it is the very condition that must precede personalism in order to culminate in it.

Here we have the beginnings of a totalizing, if not a totalitarian, form of democracy. Libertarians would be uncomfortable with such unfettered reciprocity between subject and sociality. I sing my separate self while uttering the 'En-Masse,' the body politic, yet even as I utter its name, I am, in the same breath, unable to utter it, since it precedes me and conditions me totally. Personalism, therefore, is a free self-willing toward democracy that is also, somehow, compulsorily bound to it.

'How to sing my separate self while also speaking for you, the En-Masse?' Compare Whitman's question to the rhetorical question in the final line of Ralph Ellison's *Invisible Man*. The novel concerns a young black protagonist, expelled from a Southern HBCU, who then migrates north to New York City where he gets hired as a public orator for the Communist Party in Harlem. 'Who knows,' asks the Invisible Man at the end of his tale, 'but that, on the lower frequencies, I speak for you?' At first hearing, the question sounds much like Whitman's. Yet if there is a satisfactory answer, it depends on whether, in an apparently totalized world of racist manipulation, the protagonist can find his personal path to self-acceptance and freedom. Everyone he meets in the novel—rich white philanthropists, black college presidents, Communist Party officials—wants to use him for ulterior ends without regard for his individuality. No one 'sees' him. The turning point in the novel comes when the protagonist, fleeing a riot in Harlem staged by the Communists, falls into a 'hole in the ground' from which he begins to evaluate his social misery. In this subterranean schoolhouse of sorts, he studies the art of metonymy, formulating his personal struggle in terms of humanism and democracy more generally. He sees for the first time how his present miseries were caused by the undemocratic conditions that tormented him above ground, and he decides, there and then, to realign his life with an idealized concept of democracy in which his 'humanity [would be] won by continuing to play in face of certain defeat.'

Unresolved at novel's end is what Ellison means by speaking for democracy 'on the lower frequencies.' He cannot only mean that individuals must improve their narrow self-interest into an abstract 'democratic personalism,' as Whitman contends. It seems to me that the lower frequency must also encompass the struggle for self-actualization of a young black individual who does not conceive of himself, as others in the novel would have him, primarily in terms of his race, but in terms of his own humanity, a reading for which I find support in Ellison's critical writings on American literature. In the collection titled *Shadow and Act*, for example, Ellison argues that American modernists (i.e., white writers after Mark Twain), while doing much to advance the technical aspects of fiction writing, fundamentally evaded the calling of the American writer to confront the democratic ideal in literary form, specifically the question of where American Negroes fit into the national picture of democracy. Ellison believed that nineteenth-century writers such as Whitman, Melville, and Twain viewed the black slave as a symbol of America's unrealized democratic ideal, whereas writers after World War I—Hemingway, Fitzgerald, Steinbeck—failed to consider the unfinished emancipation of the Negro as a national moral crisis. It is not that these writers did not make black characters; they did. The problem for Ellison was that they did not lend humanity to these characters by examining racial questions on a deeper moral and psychological register, by which I think he means, 'on the lower frequencies.' According to Ellison, 'The American writer has formed the habit of living and thinking in a culture that is opposed to the deep thought and feeling necessary to profound art; [hence his] precise and complex verbal constructions for converting goatsong into [a series of] carefully modulated squeaks.'

Goatsong, of course, is the meaning of the Greek word for tragedy. Recent social history was underwriting Ellison's tragic view of American literature. For him, the shortcomings of American literati reflected the social conditions out of which they arose. If the sin of segregation was institutionalized in national law and politics, then it could not but transfer to the products of high culture, even if the cultural sphere presented the greatest possibilities for democratic experimentation. The volatility of the Southern situation in particular influenced Ellison's decision to write *Invisible Man* alongside and against the American modernism of which he counted himself part. The crisis of his protagonist was the very crisis confronting Negro individuals after their Great Migration north from the Jim Crow South, a phenomenon that Ellison summarizes as follows:

> In the South, the sensibilities of both blacks and whites are inhibited by the rigidly defined environment. For the Negro there is relative safety so long as individuality is suppressed…The pre-individualistic

> black community discourages individuality out of self-defense, [having] learned through experience that the whole group is punished [corporately] for the actions of a single member.

Without reducing Ellison's novel entirely to historical allegory, the hero of *Invisible Man* might be taken as a northbound black migrant whose search for self-actualization is actually a search for the form of individuality itself. But let me be absolutely clear before I pursue this fragile point. In the above passage, Ellison is not using 'pre-individualism' as an ontological category, but as a psychological and political descriptor of the psychic damage inflicted by historical racism in the United States. I cite the term because it shows that for Ellison democratic self-willing does not begin, as it does in Whitman, with the fully self-actualized citizen, but with the socialized person living out of sight and out of earshot, prior to publicly recognized political individuality, 'on the lower frequencies.' He continues:

> It is only when the individual...rejects the pattern [of segregation] that he awakens to the nightmare of his life...[For he has forced] the Negro down into the deeper levels of [his] consciousness, into the inner world, where reason and madness mingle with hope and memory and endlessly give birth to nightmare and to dream; down into the province of the psychiatrist and the artist, from whence spring the lunatic's fantasy and the work of art. It is a dangerous region even for

> the artist, and his tragedy lies in the fact that in order to tap the fluid fire of inspiration, he must perpetually descend and reencounter not only the ghosts of his former selves, but all of the unconquered anguish of his living.

I cannot find a better summary of the themes of *Invisible Man* in all of Ellison's critical writings. The novel's Epilogue restates the above passage in a political vocabulary that emphasizes the democratic potential of the protagonist's life. Out of so-called Negro 'pre-individualism,' therefore, Ellison's hero discovers the form of the self-actualizing individuality that the underground provides him, and concludes his story, similarly to Whitman's essay, by anticipating the great democracy to come in America. Still, there is one crucial difference between Ellison's account of democratic idealism and his predecessor's. Recall that Whitman began *Leaves of Grass* with the fully self-actualized individual—'One's self I sing'—as the basis of his art of metonymy. His poetic reconciliation of transcendental individuality with mass democracy occurred by overwriting the conditions of his unemancipated reality with idealized egalitarian conditions. In the world of Ellison's novel, by contrast, readers cannot presume as operative the same egalitarian conditions we find in *Leaves of Grass*. We must instead attune our ears to the lower frequencies, seeking the transcendental underground.

In *Invisible Man*, the art of metonymy reconciles the 'pre-individualism' of the Negro protagonist with Ralph Ellison's tragic vision of American democracy. Attention should be given to how Ellison uses the word 'Negro' as a metonym that extends beyond American blacks, describing all persons who battle against external determinations that obstruct the path to liberty. Note Ellison's generalizing tone in the following quote:

> Being a Negro American involves a willed affirmation of self against all outside pressures—an identification with the group as extended through the individual self which rejects all possibilities of escape that do not involve a basic resuscitation of the original American ideals of social and political justice.

To this Ellison attaches the coy afterthought, 'And those white Negroes [could be] Negroes too—if they wish to be.' There is a strain of both negative and positive liberty in this reformulation of the word 'Negro' as a metonym that apparently refers to blacks and whites alike, the same reaching for total reconciliation of self and society that one reads in Whitman. Being Negro, for Ellison, means resisting oppressive determinations, inexhaustibly, while also willing one's mind completely in the direction of the democratic ideals of social and political justice.

III. Tragic Democracy

Between political self-mastery and value pluralism in modern Europe there was, demonstrably, an 'American art of metonymy' that emphasized the reconciliation of transcendental individuality with mass democracy. Although this distinctively American articulation contained elements of positive self-making and negative pluralism, these depended absolutely on the individual's compulsive embrace of the democratic ideal. This was equally true for Walt Whitman as for Ralph Ellison, even though the former presupposed the integrity of the individual while the latter sought through art to achieve it. At opposite ends of the 'Tragic American Century,' then, I hear resolute calls for a totalized form of democracy.

This call was necessarily distinct from those of Friedrich Schiller and Sir Isaiah Berlin, European critics who watched the modern world-historical drama from a distant province. Just as their modern accounts of democratic liberalism looked past America's domestic struggles, so the Americans I discussed looked past tragic modernity in Europe. Like Berlin, I reject the relativization of the history of ideas, but I think it is important to recognize that the political ideals of these four moderns reflected local insights and local blindnesses. Yet, even as one considers them in their plurality, the least common denominator of their writings is their definitive association of liberal democracy with the literary form of tragedy. What can our conference on literature and social justice learn from this association? At the very least, we can learn something about building up a Twenty-First-Century Democratic Idealism out of the most resilient materials available to us.

Hummingbird

Seeing the untenable symbol,
the hummingbird in your skull
fluttered backward. The nectar of your
thoughts retreated, too, until everything
that fortified you was wintered over,
your clear conscience concussed,
and you, in the freedom of your panic,
now an agent of the thrashing wings.

A moral germ was sipped to conclusion.
From then on you had to distrust
the nectar-slogging bird that drank up
symbols. It desiccated your mind's blossoms,
voiding your brain unto decisions
unsweetened by memories of the Republic's laws.
But we need you, now, to report:
once begun, did the fluttering lull?

four **FRAGMENTS**

My book, stuffed with phrases, has dropped to the floor.

—Virginia Woolf, *The Waves*

Witness

1

Orphanhood pushed you to the wharves.
The tropics promised you heartier winters,
the captain, steadier labors.

Yet the sands of far shores scalded your face
like Catalonia blizzards. Dusks confronted you
with star-clusters too abundant to scan.

2

Those orphan days were moody,
inexpressible in short-winded tongues,
leaking through your body's syntax like oil.

In your sleep you saw nothing
but fish schooling,
far as the eye could see, and
your daydreams were even poorer of world.

3

Still your memoirs grew in concentric circles
around those empty episodes, anecdotes
flocking to your mouth like gulls.

Your eyelids drew the constellations in,
revealing formations also parentless,
nudging you back to the wharves.

MICHAEL SKELTON
███ Hamilton Avenue, Apt. ███
Cincinnati, OH ███

To Whom It May Concern:

I am writing to apply for the long-term English 10 substitute at ███████ High School. To this position I bring several years' experience in writing pedagogy, my disciplinary training in literature, and a host of memories from when I sat in ████████'s English 10 classroom not ten years ago.

Since completing my graduate work in Comparative Literatures at ███████ University in New York, I have worked in the community college sector as an editor, freelance researcher, and adjunct professor of composition. Starting out in community college, where the average student's age exceeded my own, I quickly discovered that adult students expect a high level of mastery from their teachers. In trying to meet the expectations of my students, I had to raise my expectations for myself. Needless to say, being an adjunct professor has been as humbling for me as it has been affirming. Moments of triumph and moments of struggle are pretty evenly distributed in the community college classroom. What I've never had, however, are moments of ambivalence, for along with their high expectations for their teachers, my adult students bring an earnest desire to master the material for themselves.

My teaching philosophy has acquired two main points of emphasis as a result of my experiences: first, to interact with all students as equals; second, to focus on critical reading skills. Equality in the classroom is my utmost priority because it educates indirectly. The implicit goal of verbal training is prepare people to make sound judgments in public. This is another lesson I've gained from teaching adult students, who, because of their seniority to me, are much more sensitive to arbitrary exhibitions of authority. Critical reading is another priority. To significantly improve one's writing takes much longer than a single semester, thus I focus on reading skills such as comprehension, argument reconstruction, and identifying weaknesses in reasoning, all of which, if properly internalized, will follow the student for the remainder of their curriculum.

Teaching English 10 will of course present different challenges than teaching adult students. However, I am confident that my focus on learning equality and critical reading is adaptable to Mrs. ▇▇▇'s classroom, where I know these standards are already put in place. Thank you for considering my application.

Sincerely,
Michael Skelton

In Riverside Park

Between winter and spring. I am sitting on a bench facing the Hudson River, eating a baguette and a block of cheese and sipping black coffee out of a paper cup. On days I trek into the city, I eat only as much breakfast as I can carry in my hands, as I am also lugging a heavy backpack stuffed full of sweaters and books. Early mornings like this, drinking my corner-deli coffee, I feel as if I am always *in* Manhattan, haunting the diners and tunnels and parks, yet always, somehow, still a guest here, without a headquarters of my own. I am of the newest generation of tenderhearted orphans who love New York yet refuse to make the foolish sacrifices it takes to exist here month-to-month. Last night, I stayed with a friend of a friend in Brooklyn who is sponsored by her wealthy Long Island parents. Tonight, I will probably use my alumni privileges to spend the night in one of the twenty-four hour reading rooms of the ██████ University library, propping my backpack against a worktable for a pillow. I sleep at ██████ so often now that I just bring all my toiletries with me, taking shameless deodorant showers in the bathrooms, wondering each time, as I exit the library at five-thirty in the morning, whether the security guard suspects that this polite young person who always says good morning actually *lives* here. Of course, the shameful truth about my squatting is that I'm not really homeless in New York, merely precarious. I have an affordable room in a basement an hour and a half outside the city. Weeks when I bus into Manhattan, I simply squat in my former educational privilege. Sometimes I think I should be a more grateful orphan than I am, for how could I have predicted, when I was still slaving away in school, that my *alma mater* Athena would be gracious enough to provide me shelter for a lifetime?

The Geese, after Humanity

Only the geese are passportless;
briskly they commandeer the seasons.
We maligned our seasons to the coasts,
where they surrounded the vibrating rock

of our innerness with tilted glass.
Hardly were we landlocked. The rock-bottom
truth of our lives was shale-split. Currents
dissolved us into silts, dispensing us

in forests, in canyons, along
the neuro-paths of glaciers.
We layered and layered upon—and from our
compacted stillness, Science derived

perpetual motion. Yet if the geese could have
honked in our language, they would have lectured,
'You will never recognize the real eclipse.'
For they comb the coasts and inland waters;

heat and cold daily enfold them.
They roam the millennial border,
flying over it with mad urgency,
for the crossing's sake.

Excerpt from a letter to a mentor

...One beautiful thing about using the Socratic method in the classroom is that the students think that each new question is culminating in an ultimate insight. We could not be teachers if we did not succeed in preserving this illusion to some degree. I still have no idea where I was supposed to be leading the students in English 10, but I pretended that I knew, so that I would seem to them a mature thinker who had sailed to the edge of the world and back for the sole purpose of sharing my findings with them. Every student deserves a romantic first encounter with serious literature, even if he isn't serious about it himself. Otherwise, English class would just be about literacy, and the tests would have triumphed totally, instead of just mostly. The Greek etymology tells us that the way to be a philosopher is to be a 'lover of wisdom.' Perhaps this just means embracing the fool within oneself and taking the risk of *leading* the next troupe of fools into oblivion.

To tell you the truth, ▮▮▮, now that it's all over, the weight of being your substitute is hitting me with fuller force than ever. As long as I stayed occupied with work, I felt light and unburdened. But now there are no papers to grade or judgment calls to make. The students have gone home for the summer, and there is nothing left to reckon with but the eerie silence of Room 200, which, not three hours ago, was filled with voices I shall never hear again. Once I leave this room and lock the door, it is unlikely that I will ever have another gift as precious as your vocation dropped in my lap like grace. Think of how mysterious that is, how mysterious our bond now is. Our relationship could only have taken place in the public sector, where an accident of birth earned me a seat in your classroom, and an accident of fate, ten years later, earned me a seat at your desk. The symmetry is improbable. My final task as substitute is to make the symmetry mean something. I have been trying to avoid this moment since I was sixteen, the age when I first became conscious of myself as a sophomore—a 'wise fool'—seeking knowledge. No more putting it off: it is time for Skelton to become a philosopher. To do so, I must face the bitter yet liberating reality that just over three months ago, I entered a swarm of irreplaceable lives and voices and am now leaving them, instantly, as if I were never there.

Yours,
The Substitute

Dying Moths

A good literary fragment must communicate, simultaneously, economy and superabundance. Its severance from the larger work must render it capable of superseding that work, in both scope and significance.

One encounters this sort of effect all the time while reading. I am thinking of Virginia Woolf's 'Death of the Moth,' an unrevised essay published by her husband Leonard Woolf in a collection titled *The Death of the Moth and Other Essays*. That such a meager fragment was made the cornerstone of an entire collection, the first under Woolf's name after her suicide, suggests something of the magnitude of its importance.

In the essay, Woolf considers the 'queer spectacle' of a moth fluttering on the windowpane in her room. The window has a view to a pleasant September morning, 'mild, benignant, yet with a keener breath than that of the summer months.' She notes how the moth keeps an existence apart from the rest of its species. It is a 'day moth,' an anomaly going it alone, unlike its cousin the 'night moth,' a conformist who goes with the group. Woolf admits a 'queer feeling of pity' for the thing, observing that, on a keen autumn morning, when the possibilities of pleasure seem so various, it must be sad to have merely a day moth's part in life. Yet,

> [w]hat he could do he did. Watching him, it seemed as if a fibre, very thin but pure, of the enormous energy of the world had been thrust into his frail and diminutive

body. As often as he crossed the pane, I could fancy
that a thread of vital light became visible. He was little
or nothing but life.

Here Woolf is doing the only kind of mathematics that is possible in literature. The terms of her formulizing are necessarily indeterminate. How much, she asks, does a frail and diminutive body weigh against the enormous energy of the world?

Yet, because he was so small, and so simple a form of
the energy that was rolling in at the open window and
driving its way through so many narrow and intricate
corridors in my own brain and those of other human
beings, there was something marvelous as well as
pathetic about him.

The life in him is marvelous, as all life is marvelous, but the scale of life in him is, admittedly, quite pathetic. This is the turning point of the essay. The next thing that Woolf notices about the moth is that his fluttering has lost its former animation. He is becoming weaker, panicked, awkward. He falls on his back on the windowsill, exhausted from the effort of doing what just minutes before had been effortless for him. He jerks his body a few more times in protest, righting himself on his legs, then gives himself up, finally, to death:

[T]his gigantic effort on the part of an insignificant
little moth, against a power of such magnitude, to retain
what no one else valued or desired to keep, moved one
strangely…The moth having righted himself now lay

most decently and uncomplainingly composed. O yes, he seemed to say, death is stronger than I am.

These are the last lines of the essay. A magnitude has been perceived by comparing a small thing to an enormous thing, but now the small thing has died, and there is nothing more to say about it. While brief, Woolf's essay is a fine example of fragmentary writing. It reminds me of what Herman Melville once said about creating *Moby Dick*, that to write a mighty book, one must choose a mighty theme. With 'The Death of the Moth,' Virginia Woolf has chosen the mightiest of themes: the place of small versus large creatures in the community of being; the strangeness of a solitary life and death; the analogy of this strangeness, perhaps, to human existence. But the piece is so short-winded on all of these fronts that the effort seems quaint in comparison to a magnum opus like *Moby Dick*. The tome would seem indisputably greater than the fragment, and yet, in order to compute the values of the two, we would have to give up literature once for all to mathematics.

As with little moths, so with little fragments.

Essay

1

Vainly, we saluted your stature
with a sculpted swan. And we weighed
the stones in your pockets.
Shall we admit now it was all in error?

(The marble curve of the swan's neck
had a deformity
that miscarried your exhortations.)

2

Your thriving imagination demanded more
than just privacy and pounds. Foolishly,
it sought the most prudent form of dispensation
for the gross facts swelling inside it.

When the swan barked, we exhumed
your essay finally: Reality was
quaint, trumpeting, perilous.

Moving books

The rain is falling so heavily that the myriad drops seem bonded together in a single translucent curtain the color of paper. Even the sound of the rain reminds me of paper, like a thumb riffling through the pages of an old book. I am probably just imagining the effect. I am getting ready to move to Tennessee, from Ohio, and all weekend I have been handling the books in my room, sorting them, boxing them, tossing them out. How did I come to possess so many unread books? Every collector has her ways. Identifying oneself socially as a reader is the first step. Other readers suddenly become very eager to share their books and erudition with one. Many of these books belong to friends and acquaintances and need to be returned. But then, as I look at some of the on-loan titles, I suspect that I must have moved with them once or twice already, as the readers to whom they rightfully belong are now several states, or in some cases, several countries, away. A two-thirds majority, I would say, were acquired by me. Yet two-thirds of an uncountable mass is still uncountable! I was never a greedy consumer of anything until I started to take myself seriously as a reader. How many times have I gone on book-buying sprees just to boost my self-regard as an intellectual? I am not quite Gatsby. I have read a few of these books. But I am not quite Borges, either.

My problem seems to be that I have gotten ahead of myself. At some point in the past, my ambitions as a reader started to exceed my human possibilities within time and space. Was it wrong of me to desire knowledge on such an impossible scale? Only, I suppose, if I had remained unmindful of the irony that my book gathering takes as much or more time than my book reading. If I did not recognize this obvious fact, and supposed that I really did know what all my books contained, then yes, I would be a fool. But that has not been my attitude at all. I take in books like a samaritan takes in strangers. I am building a community of letters in my room. As in any public, not all of the individuals will know me well, nor I them, yet some individuals will get closer to me than others, and the rest will know they are welcome to stay with me as long as they like. My home is every author's home. My Zen is the librarian's Zen.

My method, sadly, is Linnaeus's method. Taxonomy is more important than mastery on moving day. To rightly organize a subject matter so that one can look it up later, one need only have a grasp of its general ideas. For someone like me, who keeps more books than she will ever read, the question becomes whether it is good enough to be a generalist in knowing as well as sorting. When I look at some of my philosophy books, for example, is it enough to know that the author was concerned with politics, then box him up with other political philosophers? Does that honor his contribution to the history of ideas? What if I knew that the author was a liberal individualist and not a communist? There are enough liberals in my stacks to fill their own small box, maybe two. Should I let history be my sorter, then? I have heard it said that thinkers resemble their times more than they resemble their traditions. A nineteenth-century liberal may have had more in common with a nineteenth-century socialist than he had with earlier and later liberals.

Can't I come up with a better system than this? Something between taxonomy and mastery is what I need, some course of action between collecting books and actually reading them. But if there is such a course of action, I cannot think of what it would be.

My moving-day dilemma reminds me of a day I spent with a close friend of mine about six months ago, a few weeks after his father died. The deceased was a rogue scholar and left a modest estate behind him comprised almost entirely of books. There were thousands of them, maybe even tens of thousands. There were so many books that my friend's father could not shelve them all in his little two-bedroom apartment, where he lived alone. He had to rent additional space at two different storage facilities in town, but even those ample annexes could barely subdue his collection. When my friend lifted the sliding door of one of the storage units, unopened for years, we both had to leap back to avoid the column of boxes that nearly tumbled out on our heads. Inside the unit, boxes were stacked floor to ceiling, front to back. We discovered that my friend's father had labeled them all in alphabetical order according to discipline. A typical box read, 'Soc/Econ, A-B,' although it did not take us long to find one that contradicted it, a 'Soc/Econ, A-D,' or an 'Econ/Poly, A.' The books had so multiplied over the years that their original categories could no longer describe them. Similarly exhausted labels existed for history, poetry, technology, psychology. It took us less than an hour to give up our plan of making a catalogue of every book in the estate. We agreed it was enough simply to get the boxes out of storage and haul them back to his father's apartment, where my friend, who was to be the sole executor of the books, would decide what their fates should be.

Indeed, with a lifelong book collector like my friend's father, one never makes it to the taxonomy stage, let alone the mastery stage, of book ownership. One can only shoulder one's books, as so much weight, from one place to the next, following the practical biddings of one's life. But this begs the question of why any individual (myself included) would want to possess so many disparately themed books, knowing that a mortal life could not possibly provide him enough time to read them all? This question, I think, weighed more heavily upon me that day than the books themselves. It was hard to imagine even Harold Bloom, the Olympian reader of his generation, making it to the end of all those intimidating treatises on the principles of political economy, the working classes in Victorian literature, the military coup in Chile. A person with so many titles in his possession could not possibly have been seeking clarity from his reading. On the contrary, he must have been building a monument to confusion—a confusion of the noblest kind, I should qualify, the kind that cannot be satisfied by any ideological dogma; the kind that is dissatisfied, even, with its own wisdoms.

It seemed the only immediate truth in those mountains of books was their sheer aggregate mass. Indeed, the effort of skimming through them, after so many hours of hauling them around, caused me more anxiety than pleasure. How could anyone ever contrive a system that tallied them all? How could one know even an infinitesimal fraction of the possibilities their titles represented? My grief for my friend's father increased with each subsequent box I unsealed, not because I was overwhelmed by what the two of us would never have time to know, but because I was overwhelmed by the seeming impossibility of our knowing anything at all.

At the end of the day, it gave us far more consolation to remember the man who left behind the books—his passion for music and politics, his wild beard, his love for American poetry—than to assume stewardship over his books ourselves. Although I cannot pretend to speak for my friend's state of mind that day, I for my part experienced an incredible catharsis when he finally decided to yield to the mystery of his father's estate, silencing, at least for the moment at hand, the clamoring of a thousand unopened books.

TEXTS CITED

Berlin, Isaiah. *The Crooked Timber of Humanity*. Alfred A. Knopf, New York: 1991.

—*Four Essays on Liberty*. Oxford, London: 1969.

Coetzee, J.M. *Disgrace*. Penguin Books, New York: 1999.

Ellison, Ralph. *Invisible Man*. Vintage International, New York: 1980.

—*Collected Essays of Ralph Ellison*. Edited by John Callahan. Modern American Library, New York: 1995.

Descartes, René. *Meditations on First Philosophy*. Hackett Publishing Company, Indianapolis: 1993.

Gramsci, Antonio. *Selections from the Prison Notebooks*. Edited and translated by Quintin Hoare and Geoffrey Nowell Smith. International Publishers Company, New York: 1978.

Hume, David. *A Treatise of Human Nature*. Oxford, London: 1978.

Kant, Immanuel. *Critique of Pure Reason*. Translated by N.K. Smith. Macmillan & Co.: 1929.

Keats, John. 'To Autumn.' From *Poets.org*. http://www.poets.org/poetsorg/poem/autumn.

Merton, Thomas. *Selected Poems*. New Directions, New York: 1967.

Mill, J.S. *Autobiography*. Penguin Classics, New York: 1989.

Orwell, George. 'Shooting an Elephant.' From *The Literature Network*. http://www.online-literature.com/orwell/887/

Schiller, Friedrich. *On the Aesthetic Education of Man*. Translated by Reginald Snell. Yale University Press, New Haven: 1954.

Stevens, Wallace. *The Collected Poems*. Vintage Books, New York: 1982.

Thoreau, Henry D. *Walden and Civil Disobedience*. Barnes and Noble Classics, New York: 2003.

Weil, Simone. *Gravity and Grace*. Ark Publishing, Great Britain: 1987.

Whitman, Walt. 'Democratic Vistas.' In *Leaves of Grass and Selected Prose*. Rinehart & Company, New York: 1949.

Woolf, Virginia. *A Room of One's Own*. Harcourt Brace, New York: 1981.

—*Collected Essays*. Houghton Mifflin Harcourt Publishing Company, New York: 2009.

—*Death of the Moth and Other Essays*. Harcourt Brace, New York: 1974.

—*Jacob's Room & The Waves: Two Complete Novels*. Harcourt, Brace & World, New York: 1959.

Acknowledgments

My parents, for their constancy of love and support during my meandering twenties; my sisters, for their faith and encouragement since childhood; my grandparents, for preparing the way for education; EMT, for being good company and respecting my need for solitude; my friends in Bethlehem (MG, DB, HT, AD, SOM, EG), for treating me like a bona fide local; my friends in Cincinnati (JB, KS, VT, JH, DJ), for reading with me on Wednesday nights; my friends in Columbus (JA, EB, MS, JM, MRC, CC, RT), for Monday nights; my friends from Granville, for being dynamic people from a stable place; my former colleagues (EBS, JH, NE, et al), for mentoring a naive substitute; my former teachers (JD, BT, GCS), whose lessons continue to bear fruit in this book; the many kind souls who have taken care of me in New York (especially WW); my new friends in Nashville, who are keeping philosophy alive for me; and last but not least, my deific square of democratic artists (FS, WW, VW, RE), for their astonishing visions of what a literary vocation could be.

www.ingramcontent.com/pod-product-compliance
Lightning Source LLC
Chambersburg PA
CBHW022116040426
42450CB00006B/729